Thinking Sex with the Great Whore

Many scholars in Biblical and Revelation studies have written at length about the imperial and patriarchal implications of the figure of the Whore of Babylon. However, much of the focus has been on the links to the Roman Empire and ancient attitudes towards gender. This book adds another layer to the conversation around this evocative figure by pursuing an ideological critique of the Great Whore that takes into account contemporary understandings of sexuality, and in so doing advances a de-moralization of apparent sexual deviancy both in the present and in the past.

Offering an emancipatory reading of Revelation 17–18 using Foucauldian, postcolonial, and queer historiographies, this study sets out alternative paths for identity construction in Biblical texts. By using these alternative critical lenses, the author argues that the common neglect of the ethical and political impact of Biblical texts in the present can be overcome. This, in turn, allows for fresh reflection on the study of the Bible and its implications for progressive politics.

Situated at the intersection of Revelation Studies, Biblical Studies, and Hermeneutics, as well as Contextual/Liberationist Theologies and Queer and Postcolonial Criticism, this is a cutting-edge study that will be of keen interest to scholars of Theology and Religious Studies.

Luis Menéndez-Antuña is Assistant Professor of New Testament at the Pacific Lutheran Theological Seminary and at the Graduate Theological Union (Berkeley, California). His interests revolve around Postcolonial, Critical Race and Queer Theories as well as Liberation Hermeneutics. He has published peer-reviewed contributions both in Spanish (*Theologica Xaveriana, Revista de Ciencias de Religiones*) and in English (*Biblical Interpretation, Journal of Religious Ethics, Early Christianity, Critical Research on Religion*).

Routledge Interdisciplinary Perspectives on Biblical Criticism

The Routledge Interdisciplinary Perspectives on Biblical Criticism (RIPBC) series features volumes that engage substantially with Biblical literature from perspectives not traditionally associated with Biblical studies. This series aims at employing the best tools, theories, and insights from the sciences, philosophy, and beyond to yield fresh and demonstrable insights from the Biblical texts and from Biblical criticism itself.

Volumes in this series will typically have a dual emphasis between a field of study and Biblical scholarship, and accomplish at least one of the following:

* Demonstrate why a particular field of study enables new insights in reading select biblical passages, texts, or corpora
* Show how Biblical texts have anticipated themes and issues later approached in other disciplines, and can serve as an ancient conversation partner, or prescient critique, of those areas of study
* Explain how a field of study offers a parallel insight into the methods or findings of Biblical criticism

Biblical Narratives of Israelites and Their Neighbors
Strangers at the Gate
Adriane Leveen

Cain, Abel, and the Politics of God
An Agambenian Reading of Genesis 4:1–16
Julián Andrés González Holguín

Epistemology and Biblical Theology
From the Pentateuch to Mark's Gospel
Dru Johnson

Thinking Sex with the Great Whore
Deviant Sexualities and Empire in the Book of Revelation
Luis Menéndez-Antuña

For more information about this series, please visit: www.routledge.com/religion/series/RIPBC

Thinking Sex with the Great Whore

Deviant Sexualities and Empire in the Book of Revelation

Luis Menéndez-Antuña

Routledge
Taylor & Francis Group

LONDON AND NEW YORK

First published 2018
by Routledge
2 Park Square, Milton Park, Abingdon, Oxon OX14 4RN

and by Routledge
711 Third Avenue, New York, NY 10017

Routledge is an imprint of the Taylor & Francis Group, an informa business

© 2018 Luis Menéndez-Antuña

British Library Cataloguing-in-Publication Data
A catalogue record for this book is available from the British Library

Library of Congress Cataloging-in-Publication Data
Names: Menéndez-Antuña, Luis, author.
Title: Thinking sex with the great whore : deviant sexualities and
   empire in the Book of Revelation / Luis Menéndez-Antuña.
Description: New York : Routledge, 2018. | Series: Routledge
   interdisciplinary perspectives on biblical criticism | Includes
   bibliographical references and index.
Identifiers: LCCN 2018001283 | ISBN 9781138306998 (hardback :
   alk. paper) | ISBN 9781315142166 (ebook)
Subjects: LCSH: Sex—Biblical teaching. | Bible. Revelation,
   XVII-XVIII—Criticism, interpretation, etc.
Classification: LCC BS2825.6.S6 M46 2018 | DDC 228/.06—dc23
LC record available at https://lccn.loc.gov/2018001283

ISBN: 978-1-138-30699-8 (hbk)
ISBN: 978-1-315-14216-6 (ebk)

Typeset in Sabon
by Apex CoVantage, LLC

Contents

Acknowledgments

It takes a village to raise a child. This child arrived to the United States a few years ago in search for some wisdom, and found a village full of wise, caring, and supportive villagers. I would like to thank Professor Fernando Segovia for his mentorship, intellectual and personal friendship. Fernando embodies what it means to be intellectually rigorous and theoretically engaging and, more importantly, how to be kind, supportive, and respectful in these troubling times. Elena, qué te voy a decir que no sepas, te adoro y siempre estaré en deuda contigo por tu apoyo. Mi aspiración es que pueda ser para otros estudiantes lo que tú has sido para mí.

Professor Ellen Armour was most supportive and patient in teaching this child the intricacies of theory. Ellen, thanks for keeping your office open, for kindly enduring my struggles with psychoanalysis, and for always saying yes to my requests. Professor Daniel Patte and Kathy Gaça, thank you for your respectful reading of the manuscript, and for your insightful critiques.

Several institutions helped this child to write the project. First, Fulbright provided me with the unique opportunity of enrolling in the doctoral programs of my dreams. Second, Vanderbilt Divinity School provided a home and generous funding to complete the project. The Robert Penn Warren Center for Humanities offered a second home to discuss many parts of the book. Mona Frederick and Terry Tripp thanks for opening those doors. My cohort at the Robert Penn Warren Center, Jessica Burch, Adam Burgos, Daniel McAuley, Kathleen DeGuzman, Carly Rush, Amy Tan, and Brendan Weaver read different versions of the manuscript and offered invaluable critiques. I could not have finished the project without the unconditional support of the Hispanic Theological Initiative. Joanne Rodríguez, eternamente agradecido. Ángela Schoepf, siempre tan disponible. Gracias especialmente a mis amigos de HTI por demostrarme cada semana qué significa ser y estar en conjunto: Xochitl Alvizo, Julián González, Manuela Ceballos, qué linda gente.

I would also like to thank my graduate assistants, Cassandra Chávez, Nikkeya Berryhill, and Janet Katari, for their invaluable time sorting out bibliographical and formatting minutiae. So thankful for your help and good disposition.

Gracias a mamá, papá, Raquel y Adauto, y a James, for keeping the flame of life alive.

1   Thinking resistance in the age of empire
Ethical evaluations of the apocalypse of John

Introduction

After the description of the Whore and the Beast in Revelation 17, Chapter 18 shows the "Fall of Babylon," and the effects of her demise on those who have had interactions with her. If Babylon/the Whore equals Rome, as scholars unanimously agree, then 18:8 expresses the community's desire to see Empire destroyed by the hand of the strong God. The woman/territory that shall burn in fire (ἐν πυρὶ κατακαυθήσεται) conjures – in Western culture – images of women being burnt because of their allegedly surreptitious power, as well as of nations scorched for their resistance to submit to imperialism. The fact that it is a strong Lord God who judges her justifies the cause of her burning, as is to be expected in apocalyptic literature, on religious/theological grounds. This is not to say that the trope of women/nations in need being destroyed because of their evil actions has its origin in Revelation, but it is to say that the Apocalypse of John is part of a long tradition (biblical and non-biblical) where the gendered, sexualized, and colonized Other must be destroyed, punished, or disciplined. It is no wonder, then, that, given the cultural influence of the Bible in general, and the Apocalypse in particular, Revelation scholars always make reference to the message's applicability to the present.

This chapter is designed as an entry point to understanding the methodological assumptions and hermeneutical moves that contemporary scholarship carries out when dealing with the impact of Revelation's critique of Empire through the image of the Whore. The chapter starts precisely delineating this problem: how different paradigms of interpretation have tackled the issue of the relationship of Revelation to the Roman Empire. The presentation is, however, guided by a contemporary ideological concern in that my goal is to see how those same positions are applied to the present. To put it simply, biblical scholars' concern with the past is presented, analyzed, and criticized from my own concern for the present – for the potential use of Revelation for emancipatory purposes.

Overview: ethical assessments of Revelation in terms of empire

The relationship between John's Apocalypse and the Roman Empire has been studied since the second century.[1] Revelation's stance towards the Roman Empire, its ethical and political evaluation as pro- or anti-imperial literature, has centered recent scholarly debates in Revelation Studies. The so-called "ethical turn" in Biblical Studies provides the context for such inquiry in that scholars are concerned about the sociological, cultural, political, theological, and ideological effects of bringing past texts to the present.[2] Regarding the Apocalypse of John, scholarship is concerned about the work's emancipatory potential for its (Roman Empire) and our own (Present Empire) context.

Revelation has been read throughout history in very different ways, from a literary and theological source legitimating the *status quo* to ideological fodder for radical emancipatory movements. Whether such interpretations come from the secular or the religious, the a-confessional or the theological, the popular or the academic, the ideological or the political – Revelation is a controversial book. The "ethical turn" has been especially sharp at pointing at the ambiguous consequences of appropriating Revelation's emancipatory potential for our times by way of reflecting on the book's stance toward the Roman Empire. Contemporary interpreters who focus on the question of power reflect on the identity formation of a minority religious group in the midst of the Roman Empire, bringing to the fore the group's resistant strategies to cope with mainstream culture, but also pointing out the ways in which such resistance plays into the hands of the imperial ideology – especially when it comes to gender configurations. Consequently, the ethical turn reflects on the historical conditions that made liberation and resistance possible in the first century.

Such a project has been carried out in a threefold way: 1) Textual, Literary, and Sociological approaches concern themselves with the first-century milieu contextualizing Revelation in terms of its Roman and Jewish setting; 2) Empire Studies pursue a similar strategy by stressing the oppositional relationship between a Christian minority and the Imperial reality; and 3) Liberation and ideological criticisms conceive of Revelation as an archive that foregrounds or supplements a reflection on the ethical, the political, and the ideological realms both in the present and in the past. All of these approaches concern themselves with the relevance of the apocalyptic in the present, although only Liberation and Ideological Studies have partially pursued a methodological reflection on historiography as a way to theorize the biblical grasp on the present, and on power and agency as notions worthy of critical survey in the present Empire.

In the following, I present approaches to the question of apocalyptic resistance to Empire from all of the above-mentioned approaches. The organization of the material follows ideological criteria, rather than methodological. After briefly introducing the problematic at hand (Empire and

Revelation), I present the scholarship by Adela Yarbro Collins and Elisabeth Schüssler Fiorenza as two representatives of the positions that will be analyzed throughout the chapter. Whereas the first author views Revelation as promoting an ultimately inefficient ethics of resistance – what I call "Revelation complicit with Empire" – the second considers Revelation the paradigmatic example of emancipatory politics ("Revelation against Empire"). Both scholars are also exemplary representatives of the methodological/theoretical complexity within Revelation Studies. While Yarbro Collins advocates for historical-critical literary approaches to the text, Schüssler Fiorenza has decisively contributed to the shaping of ideological approaches.

These scholars' broad concern with the positioning of Revelation within Imperial politics frames the more specific topic of the representation of Empire through the gendered/sexualized trope of Babylon/the Great Whore. The two main sections in the first part of the chapter ("Revelation versus Empire" and "Revelation complicit with Empire") unfold as expected and focused expansions of these two original positions. I approach these developments with two concerns in mind: First, the ideological underpinning of presenting Empire through the trope of the Whore and second, the consequential effects for the present political context of such diverse understandings of the biblical texts. Consequently, the second part of the chapter concludes by summarizing the main insights from the scholarship into these two concerns and pointing at the problematic aspects of the arguments presented. Specific aspects of such problematizing find its resolution in the following chapters.

Revelation and empire

When it comes to pitting Christianity against Empire, scholars have traditionally classified New Testament writings along a continuum, with rebellion and compliance on opposite ends.[3] That same scholarship usually considers Revelation to be the most anti-imperial biblical document. Recent works have contested such agreement by exposing the ways in which resistance is co-opted by the status quo.

Historical-critical, literary, and sociological approaches share an understanding of Revelation as oppositional to Empire. Similarly, Liberation exegesis entirely adheres to such evaluation as it draws conclusions for our present political context,[4] taking the book as a charter document for the unsettlement of the *status quo* in the context both of Imperium and of global capitalism.[5] In the following, I introduce the works by Adela Yarbro Collins and Elisabeth Schüssler Fiorenza as an entry point to survey the wide range of interpretations that, from very different methodological perspectives, conceive of Revelation as literature that either opposes or is complicit with Empire.

Both authors have shaped the debate about the ethical and political import of Revelation since the end of the 1970s. Their contribution remains relevant and it is paradigmatic of different methodological positions that result in oppositional evaluations. In the following, I will present in detail their arguments as paradigmatic examples of "Revelation against Empire," and "Revelation complicit with Empire," and as an introductory venue to map more recent theoretical developments in Revelation Studies that address the emancipatory potential of the Apocalypse of John.

Revelation as "ultimately" complicit with empire: Adela Yarbro Collins

Yarbro Collins was one of the first scholars to suggest that there were no systematic prosecutions directed against Christians and that consequently Revelation could not be conceived as addressing an "empirical" reality as much as a "perceived crisis." Revelation, she said, is a "response to a perceived crisis,"[6] an attempt to hinder any Christian involvement with Imperial ideology in terms of religion, wealth, and gender.[7] Yarbro Collins understands Revelation's oppositional stance as deriving from inner communitarian conflicts between two parties: John and his uncompromising position towards Empire on one side,[8] and his adversaries who seek a compromise with Empire as a way to live comfortably on the other. Among these, Jezebel and Balaam would represent an accommodating branch of Christianity that questions John's authority and his countercultural position. While the seer seeks a radical disengagement from civil society and Roman religious cults, Jezebel represents those Christians who aspire to live peacefully in the midst of Imperium. Using Niebuhr's terminology, Jezebel advocates a "Christ embracing culture" while John defends a "Christ against culture."[9]

Yarbro Collins argues that Revelation's attack on Empire does not come from a material or historical persecution as much as from a tension between two value systems,[10] two cosmovisions that collide at economical, religious, and social levels. Revelation represents an attempt to promote social radicalism by way of building a symbolic system that, on the one side, represents an alternative kingdom and, on the other, can help Christians to cope with aggressive feelings that derive from their marginal social situation.[11] The radical nature of Revelation is best appreciated in its oppositional stance towards Rome's economic rule. Yarbro Collins interprets the χάραγμα (Rev 13:16–17) as a sign of exclusivism – as a call to skip the imperial economy not because John considers wealth to be an intrinsic evil,[12] but because it perpetuates the Roman rule by participating in its trade. John's uncompromising approach is rooted, according to Yarbro Collins, in his own religious beliefs, but it has religious, political, economic, and cultural consequences. For Yarbro Collins, Revelation is a response to a perceived crisis that, due to the expectation of an imminent judgment, seeks to trigger a response from its audience of total withdrawal from Empire.[13]

Religious conflict triggers a series of economic and social measures that isolate the Christian group from its immediate context, which, in turn, ends up causing despair among the believers. Revelation functions as an antidote to the perceived contradiction between reality and expectation,[14] simultaneously providing the diagnosis and the cure. The cathartic experience of allowing the audience to witness the demise of the present world while envisioning a utopian realm empowers believers not to succumb to a perceived overwhelmingly oppressive reality. The apocalyptic genre is empowering in itself for it mitigates feelings of powerlessness by providing privileged information of heavenly origin,[15] repeated over and over so as to confirm that the fate of the adversaries is imminent and bleak. Yarbro Collins reads the dichotomous and Manichean cosmovision as John's strategy to comfort his listeners that there is a different, more important, and ultimate reality that trumps the present one.[16] Such a strategy works, however, against a cohesive resistant strategy because it resolves the tension only at the imaginative level, not materially or historically.[17]

Babylon/the Great Whore, as an anti-imperial trope, serves the rhetorical purposes of Revelation because, on one side, it summarizes Rome's evil traits at many levels and, on the other, her demise symbolizes the breakdown of the world she stands for.[18] In Yarbro Collins's view there are four reasons that explain Babylon's doom: 1) the idolatrous and blasphemous worship offered and encouraged by Rome, especially the emperor cult; (2) the violence perpetrated by Rome, especially against Jews and Christians; (3) Rome's blasphemous self-glorification; and (4) Roman wealth.[19] Babylon's doom allows the audience to overcome the frustration derived from these circumstances by making a spectacle out of her demise and by staging the tears of those who worshipped and traded with her.[20] Yarbro Collins consistently interprets Babylon/the Great Whore as a metaphor that stands for Empire without analyzing the gendered/sexualized aspects of the image. John's misogyny is most apparent in Rev 14:4, where John's concern for purity, as a phenomenon rooted in a negative attitude towards the body, is symptomatic of his attempt to navigate the psychological effects of Imperium. For Yarbro Collins, Revelation's stance towards sexual intercourse and towards women is an effect of John's conception of the body as vulnerable.

If Revelation's overall message is interpreted as a cathartic experience for the audience, the author's gender and sexual imaginary is viewed as rooted in a schizophrenic-like mindset. Yarbro Collins reminds us of Ernest Becker's theory on how the schizophrenic person regards his or her body as something that "happened" to him or her, as a mass of stench and decay. This is very important because, due to the traditional identification between the material aspects of the body with the feminine, Revelation's imaginary fosters injustice towards women and certain alienation from the body.[21] Furthermore, John's male-dominated world is inspired in the world of the Essenes and consequently rooted in the Jewish tradition where priests and warriors were male (1:6; 5:10).[22] This explains why John envisions the struggle with Rome as a Holy War in which Christians are called to remain pure. From this perspective, the demise of the Great Whore reassures Christians in their final victory as it channels their aggressive impulse towards the imaginative realm.[23]

Yarbro Collins is concerned with the ways in which Revelation's aggressive impulses and misogyny may play a role in the present, especially in the life of the Church through the reading of the authoritative text. In her essay on Women's History, Yarbro Collins acknowledges the ambivalent value that the Bible in general and Revelation in particular have for the emancipation of women. On the one hand, Revelation is a record of oppression, but, on the other, it is an authoritative text that remains a source for "a usable past" and for "images of hope."[24] Revelation's language is thoroughly androcentric and therefore calls for an ethical reflection of its gender bias.

Yarbro Collins evaluates John's resistant strategy both in its historical context and in its virtual applicability for the present. Regarding the Roman context, Yarbro Collins argues that catharsis works because it defuses pathological behavior by way of acknowledging the experienced crisis and by not "making it worse." Catharsis is also a fitting response because it does not encourage direct violence against neighbors which, given the situation of the minority group, would have daunting consequences.[25] However, Yarbro Collins warns, Revelation gives up the idea of sociopolitical transformation by discouraging activism and by postponing utopia to heavenly time. To put it simply, Revelation works at the psychological level in that it helps Christians to come to terms with an overbearing oppressive reality, but it is politically ineffective in that it transposes any effective action from the real world onto the theological.

Furthermore, Yarbro Collins is critical of hermeneutical approaches that try to analogously apply Revelation's solution for the present. Such a "precritical response"[26] is to be supplemented by a Christianized actualization of Revelation's strategies. She states that "as criteria for assessing the political stance and relational tone of the Apocalypse I propose the values of humanization, justice, and love."[27] While acknowledging Schüssler Fiorenza's argument that it is easy to dismiss Revelation's aggressive feelings when interpreters do not suffer oppression or are not involved in a continuous struggle for justice, Yarbro Collins considers that Revelation's intrinsically dualistic symbolic system, which does not abide by the proposed theological criteria for stigmatizing the other, is a failure in love.[28] No anti-imperial strategy can be recovered nowadays because there is no specific program in the book dealing with the reality of Empire as such.

On the positive side, Revelation seems to encourage a trend in contemporary Liberation theologies that consider that collective issues must be dealt with collectively. Revelation supports the current trend in which the churches take public stands on social issues, a trend that is well established in the mainline Protestant churches, reviving in evangelical and fundamentalist circles, and now spreading to the Roman Catholic Church. Yarbro

Collins sees the political theology of Metz as a promising way of putting the imperative of revelation into action. Metz proposes that the church be an "institution of a socially critical freedom" that avoids the tendency to be a "ghetto-society" or a "protective shell" for the existing society. Revelation then can help the church in its task of unmasking the pretensions of ideologies by "naming the beast," and its alliance with those tendencies in society that hold promise of a movement forward toward the fulfillment of the eschatological promises of the Bible. The ambiguous value of Revelation for the present also extends to virtual appropriations of its gendered and sexual imagery. For Yarbro Collins, "all the feminine symbols of Revelation are ambiguous when viewed from the point of view of the desirability of mutuality between men and women, and of the flexibility in the definition of male and female roles."[29]

Revelation as "definitely" resistant to empire: Elisabeth Schüssler Fiorenza

Elisabeth Schüssler Fiorenza has most notably theorized Revelation as the book where, to use Friesen's words, "the lines between God's people and the rest of the world are drawn more clearly, the opponents are chastised more thoroughly, and the final destruction of evil is more central."[30] Unlike any other theorist, Schüssler Fiorenza relates Revelation to recent theoretical developments in the discipline of Biblical Studies and advocates a critical-emancipatory hermeneutic that conceives of Revelation as a template for resistance to Empire in the present. For Schüssler Fiorenza, Revelation zeroes in on the following question: Who is the Lord of this World? To this, John responds: God and only God. Such a theological answer has crucial subversive political and economic consequences in that it questions imperial structures in place and proposes a plan for activism in the past and in the present. Revelation constitutes a "fitting response" to a given historical milieu[31] by providing a way out of an oppressive system for those who hunger and thirst for justice.[32] The Apocalypse is, in the end, a phantasy designed to transform the world in which Christians live by encouraging them to resist oppression.

Schüssler Fiorenza faults those who see Revelation as a misogynist text for essentializing gender as a category of analysis and, consequently, mistaking imagery for reality (Babylon is not a real woman). For Schüssler Fiorenza, the city stands as a figure of the evil nature of Empire, not as a representation of the whorish nature of a real woman.[33] She acknowledges that God and the Lamb inhere in the power rhetoric that legitimizes the Emperor's position, and that the heavenly court and the war waged between the chosen and the enemies, if interpreted naively, might play into the hands of Imperium. However, and despite such replication, she insists that Revelation crafts an emancipatory rhetoric that appeals to the downtrodden in the struggles against oppression.

The heavenly Jerusalem stands as the symbolic alternative to Imperial destruction, as a locus of hope for the oppressed, and as a utopian space that consequently resembles Schüssler Fiorenza's theorization of biblical discipline as a radical democratic space, as a symbol that – ideally – integrates personal, political, cultural, social, and theological splits.[34] This apocalyptic space is construed as an antidote to kyriarchy. This concept is probably Schüssler Fiorenza's most influential contribution both for Biblical Studies and Revelation. Given the importance of Empire, gender, and sexuality in my project, it is important to discuss in detail the notion of "kyriarchy" and its implication both for the analysis of the biblical text and for what it means in the context of the present Empire.

Schüssler Fiorenza coins the term *kyriarchy* to refer to the power pyramid in place in the Greco-Roman society in which the rule of the emperor, lord, slave-master, husband, and the elite freeborn, propertied, educated gentleman demanded the existence of a disenfranchised wo/men class that stood subordinated. This understanding is not abstract and ahistorical, nor temporal or totally contextual. Schüssler Fiorenza understands it as a heuristic concept that analyzes the interdependence of identitarian categories (gender, race, class, etc.), their discursive formations, and their embodied expressions. Accordingly, kyriarchy scans through times and places what factors are predominant and how they relate to each other.[35] Kyriarchy differs from patriarchy as a heuristic concept in that it is multidimensional and does not take gender as the primary point of investigation. Schüssler Fiorenza suggests that postcolonial, liberation, Marxist, and European feminist critics have failed to acknowledge how oppression works at different levels and consequently have contributed to masking the "complex interstructuring of kyriarchal dominations inscribed in the subject positions of individual wo/men and in the status positions of dominance and subordination between wo/men. They also mask the participation of white elite wo/men – or better, 'ladies'."[36] Consequently, the destruction of Babylon – contra Pippin or Moore – as a gendered figure is not to be grieved by wo/men, because that would imply an ascription on behalf of the interpreter to the ideology of the White Lady. Why, she asks, would not subaltern wo/men rejoice in the downfall of the imperial power, even if portrayed in terms of the feminine?[37] Such a question raises the problematic of how contemporary oppressed communities should read Revelation, particularly the figure of the Great Whore. For Schüssler Fiorenza Revelation's fitting response can be adequately translated into the present only "wherever a social-political-religious 'tension' generated by oppression and persecution persists or re-occurs."[38] She further argues that to understand the demise of the Great Whore as misogynist buys into the ideology of the White Lady by deploying gender as the privileged category of analysis and dismissing the ways class, race, status, and so on constitute privilege.

Recapitulating: framing the debate on contemporary politics of resistance

The presentation of both scholars' arguments and concerns throws into relief the ethical import of Revelation: What for Yarbro Collins appears to be a marginal, though persistent, preoccupation for Schüssler Fiorenza is the occasion not only to theorize Revelation but the strategies of interpreting biblical texts itself. Whereas for the first author the present is of less concern, for the second "the question of our present" is the origin of her research. This difference has, as it happens, important consequences for the ways in which they present their conclusions about the Apocalypse of John. On the one hand, Yarbro Collins considers that Revelation is not politically effective (in the past) because it transfers the conflict from the realms of the historical into the imaginary, leaving the status quo in place. Furthermore, Revelation's gender ideology replicates Roman sexual mores. However, when it comes to applying the book's politics to the present, she labels "precritical" any attempt to re-appropriate resistance strategies. The question of the present, in sum, plays no role in Yarbro Collins's methodology except as an addendum. Although "Revelation complicit with Empire" will pay considerably more attention to present concerns, it shall follow Yarbro Collins's view that apocalyptic literature reinscribes imperial dynamics by not challenging the hegemonic gender system. On the other hand, for Schüssler Fiorenza the Apocalypse's resistance is applicable because it conveys a world vision from under and, more importantly, because she adopts a rhetoric-ethical approach that takes the present as its point of departure. Revelation's gender ideology is subversive and it should not be considered in essentializing terms, but as a part of interlocking strategy to resist kyriarchy.

In sum, both authors have set the debate in terms of exegetical arguments, methodological approaches, and ideological concerns. Although a straightforward identification of "Resistant Revelation" and "Complicit Apocalypse" cannot be drawn with Schüssler Fiorenza's and Collin's contributions respectively, their insights on the relationship between Revelation and Empire shall prove the starting point to reflect on the proper contextualization of Empire in the present.

Revelation versus empire

In the present section, I present approaches that follow after Schüssler Fiorenza's evaluation of the Apocalypse, and make use of some of her exegetical moves. However, they might be skeptical or reluctant to commit to an emancipatory methodology. Most of the surveyed authors fall under the rubric of the historical and literary approaches. Whereas historically oriented interpretations conceive language as referring to an outside reality, and literary methods consider language as self-contained in the text, both paradigms – unlike Schüssler Fiorenza's – skip the relationship between language and contemporary interpreter. This insight is only partially developed only in liberationist readings. My goal here, as well as in the next section, is not to provide an exhaustive list of authors, but rather offer some representative voices within the paradigms mentioned, focusing on the critique of Empire through the trope of Babylon. Consequently, I shall move chronologically from historical criticism to literary studies and finally to emancipatory readings which set up the stage for ideological positions that advocate for a "collaborationist Revelation." This is the primary focus in the next section.

G. K. Beale's monumental commentary on Revelation is the most thorough exegetical interpretation to this day, providing the basis for many other commentaries that follow that traditional format and shaping many arguments advanced from literary and sociological approaches. He defines his approach as "historical-exegetical,"[39] and argues that the main thrust in Revelation's controversy against Empire is of religious nature. John's purpose is to encourage the churches to withdraw from any cultic practice, exhorting believers "to witness to Christ in the midst of a compromising, idolatrous church and world."[40] For Beale, Revelation is religious resistance literature in the sense that every oppositional feature within the book is explained through its theological positioning against imperial cult. In this sense, Beale situates the field of contention, to put it in materialist terms, at the super-structural level. As I shall show in Chapter 4, nowhere does this interpretation of Revelation become clearer than in Revelation 17–18 where the figure of Babylon embodies the idolatrous religious system that is to be annihilated.[41] For Beale, the gendered/sexualized nature of Babylon needs to be understood in terms of John's use of the prophets who, once again, are interpreted only as anti-idolatry figures. This is not to say that Revelation, in Beale's view, does not criticize the Roman economic system. To the contrary, Babylon stands as trope against any economic-religious system (pagan or not), but the ultimate explaining factor is of a theological nature.[42]

From within the historical paradigm but incorporating epigraphy, Koester argues, unlike Beale and Aune, that "Revelation vs. Empire" is based on the wide-ranging critique of the imperial economic-political system.[43] Koester focuses on Revelation 18 to study how John deploys rhetoric in order to trigger his audience against the trading practices of Rome. Although he does not pay attention to the gendered/sexualized nature of the metaphor of Babylon, his writing reads as resistance literature that opposes two types of slavery: that of Empire and that of God. The first one is depicted in its material terms; the second one represents the belonging of the believer in the kingdom of God. Koester notes that in the historical context there was an ambivalent opinion towards slavery in general. On one side, slavery was taken for granted; on the other, different authors point out the greed and the oppressive practices of the slave traders. John is playing with this ambivalence in order to persuade his audience of the evils of imperial ideology.

Koester analyzes a stele with different panels and offers it as an intertext for reading Rev 18: the stele shows (at the bottom) the cruel reality of the slavery trade while at the top it depicts a banquet hosted and enjoyed by slave traders. Koester argues that imperial ideology is pointing at the beneficial economic effects of slave trade by situating the banquet at the top, while Revelation points its finger at the bottom part of the stele (Rev 18:23).

Whether historical-critical scholars locate resistance at the religious or the material level, they approach language as referring to a historical reality in the past. The text's relationship to the present is cut off through an objectivistic conception of meaning that skips the question of the rhetorical or political impact of the text in the present. In the studies mentioned, unlike the examples of Yarbro Collins and Schüssler Fiorenza, the political applicability for the present is not only undertheorized, but is missing altogether. Similar characteristics are found in literary approaches, although for altogether different reasons. Huber's early work is a paradigmatic example of this methodology. She focuses on the literary world of the text (especially metaphors) rather than on the political implications of John's symbolic world.[44] Her work is relevant for our purposes for two reasons: 1) Huber focuses on the metaphor of the Bride and, consequently, on the gendered/sexualized nature of Revelation's imagery; and 2) Huber's approach remains "within the text," and consequently not paying attention to the ideological, political, moral effects of the literary topos (metaphor).

Huber uses "conceptual metaphor" to explore the ways in which the literary shapes thought. Building on Ricoeur's theory, which helps her to focus on the cognitive nature of language, Huber explains in detail how the nuptial metaphor works in the Hebrew Bible and shows the overlapping connections between different images: "A city is a woman," "A woman is a bride," and so on and concludes by stressing how John is concerned with the community's identity. John presents the community as a renewed Jerusalem that comes down from heaven, as a place where God dwells. Consequently, the crafted language of metaphoricity in Revelation gears towards community shaping, as a reworking of the wedding imagery already existent in the Roman Imperium towards building a new identity or, as Huber puts it, "identity formation through metaphorical performativity."[45]

Like most literary approaches, Huber's *Like a Bride Adorned* papers over the material conditions that enable/trigger the use of literary topos but, more importantly from my perspective, in this work she pays little attention to the ideological consequences of metaphoricity. To use her own example, "Achilles is a lion" is a powerful metaphor because, building on Ricoeur, language divests itself of its function of direct description.[46] Achilles is at once the same as a lion and not a lion. A metaphor 'preserves the "is not" within the "is." Huber, agreeing with Schüssler Fiorenza, is wary of interpreting women in Revelation in exclusively gendered terms, but, by not paying attention to power in language dynamics her approach does not account for the ways in which language, though heavily drawing from tradition, modifies tradition for particular ideological purposes. Though the community sees itself, in John's words, as a bride and in a relationship of marriage with God, we need to account for what has been sacrificed in the process – what the metaphor ignores. For the bride to marry, the whore has to be killed. In a dwelling place where there is no room for prostitutes, there is no room for the sexually deviant.

A similar methodological approach can be found in Rossing's study on the literary topos of the two cities.[47] Rossing pays close attention to the ideological and political implications of the literary topoi. Accordingly, she argues that the literary topos is deeply connected to political and ideological exhortations in that the portrayal of Babylon and Jerusalem respectively, as the stereotypical evil and good woman, triggers in its audience an oppositional stance towards Rome. Rossing explores the two-woman topos both in classical and Jewish sources. Her approach has the advantage of exploring the ideological and political effects of the literary word by pointing at the way in which the author reworks the inherited tradition to his own political ends. Accordingly, Revelation's considerable achievement is to transform a wisdom topos related to personal morals into a critical trope of political and economic import. Whereas authors like Dio Chrysostom, Aristides, and Sicilius Italicus deployed in different ways the two-women topos to illustrate the contraposition between vice and virtue (very much like Prov 1–9), Revelation takes that contraposition to a whole new level by pitting two empires/cities against each other, "the one demonic and the other divine."[48]

At the literary level, Rossing argues that John takes up a metaphor and politicizes it by establishing a clear-cut dichotomy between two empires. Babylon presents itself as a prostitute for the purposes of expanding Rome's imperial critique. For Rossing, the prostitute is a "fitting" topos to show how Rome enriches itself at the expense of the colonized peoples, and to illustrate the allure of power. Consequently, the prostitute is not so much a deviant sexual persona as much as a political figure. Therefore, the punishment of Babylon in 17:16 is not an assault on and exposure of a woman's body, but a trope for the destruction of the city, and ultimately, of the Roman Empire. The call to get out of Rome symbolizes John's stance against participating in the Roman economy. In the end, Rossing interprets Revelation's dual imagery as a political option whereby the audience needs to choose between what is good and evil. The New Jerusalem/the Bride embodies the perfect and only alternative to the "toxic Babylon/Rome's imperialism, violence, unfettered commerce, and injustice."[49]

Whereas in the previous reading the Great Whore stands "for something else," for Marshall, Babylon is located at the crossroads of the colonizer-colonized relationship. Revelation is accordingly a product of the colonizer/colonized relationship and, consequently, Babylon is the gendered/sexualized manifestation of an identity clash. Marshall takes Revelation's contempt for women as fact and explains it by identifying gender politics as a consequence of a subaltern identity. The sexualized violence against female figures both within and without his community is a function of John's position as a resister written within a situation of colonialism. Anti-colonial ideology and male chauvinism are the two sides of a coin.[50] The contrast between Jezebel and Babylon, on the one hand, and the Queen of Heaven and the Lamb/Bride, on the other, is between an active and a passive woman, between impure and pure, between the woman condemned by god to suffer sexual violence and the woman protected from it by divine and male power, between the woman engaged in human political and cultural contest and the woman on whose behalf a man acts, and ultimately between the whore and the virginal idealized mother. This dichotomy is informed, in Marshall's understanding, by John's concern with purity.

Matthews goes a step further and argues that Revelation is not against the Roman Empire, but against this world altogether. In his opinion, Revelation is not so much against the injustice of the imperial system as wary of any earthly solution that redeems the present age. The final (only) solution is the intervention of Christ with his vindication of the faithful and the elimination of the wealthy.[51] In Matthews's view, the Apocalypse is a theological template designed to resist any earthly kingdom that does not abide by supposedly Christian standards. Revelation represents the point of departure from this world into the utopian Christian kingdom that, in turn, abrogates any power demand from the earthly rule.

A similar position can be found in those approaches that seek to locate Revelation within specific geopolitical contexts. Usually inspired by liberationist ethics, contextual readings establish a parallelism between Revelation's anti-imperial stance and contemporary resistant movements against capitalism and Empire. *From Every People and Nation* is a paradigmatic example of this kind of reading. David Rhoads introduces the work by biographically contextualizing his own work and then by proceeding to introduce cultural interpretation within the field of Biblical Studies. Cultural interpretation "includes the theories, strategies, practices, and results of interpreting the Bible self-consciously out of one's cultural location" whose goal is "to foster justice, transformation, and liberation through the process of interpretation."[52] Rhoads then explains the main tenets of a proper contextual reading, underscoring the necessity of paying attention to power dynamics at the level of the biblical text per se – the relationship between interpreter-text, interpreter-interpreter, and interpreter-communities of interpretation. Properly, the interpretations are not offered as definite interpretations, but as intervention in service of the communities interpreters belong to.

Interpreters deploying contextual/cultural hermeneutics tend to stress the plight of the communities they stand for. For instance, Brian Blount shows how, from an African-American perspective, Revelation is read by and for that community as a script of resistance and anti-accommodation to dominant culture, especially by the lure that such culture has for some middle and upper-class persons. Revelation makes sense only "from below." Otherwise, it will be construed as hateful or envious. The position adopted by the interpreter ("from below") is the hermeneutical lens that allows for a cross-historical application.[53]

Gonzalez, for his part, pays attention to the ambiguous position of living at the center of the Empire, simultaneously oppressed and allured by its enchantments. He reconstructs a historical setting where Christianity is an oppressed way of living that reminds contemporary Christians of their paradoxical existence at the heart of Empire. Revelation's ethical import comes from its warning that Christian identity demands total alliance: "we are ambivalent about Revelation because we are ambivalent about our discipleship."[54]

Clarice Martin offers a womanist reading of Revelation, taking the experience of slavery as her point of departure and reading Rev 18:11–13 with its reference to "slaves and human lives," as a key element in John's anti-imperial stance. Theoretically, Martin foregrounds her interpretation on a contextual womanist approach that takes Alice Walker's insights as a lens to explore the emancipatory potential in the book focusing primarily on John's "sharply polemical indictment of the pervasive and baleful commodification and trafficking of human beings throughout the Roman Empire."[55] Martin starts her study by noting dissimilarities between the ancient slavery system (there was no racialization) and similarities (total domination, social death, and dishonor). Martin understands Revelation as a "minority report," that rejects the worldview of the "cognitive majority."[56]

In sum, literary approaches that ascribe themselves to linguistic theories of metaphoricity (Huber) or intertextuality (Rossing), similarly to historical-critical approaches, forego the question of the present. This is all the more surprising considering the influence that Schüssler Fiorenza has on them. To the contrary, literary approaches that adopt liberationist strategies of interpretation tackle the question of the present by theorizing the role of the interpreter/reader in the act of interpretation or by situating their interpretation in specific contexts. The historiographical question of the relationship between past and present is, however, pervasively undertheorized.

Revelation complicit with empire

Scholars who advocate a "Revelation complicit with Empire" are concerned with the ways resistance is implicated with power. John's proposal, as the argument goes, despite seeking to build a discourse at the margins and against Empire, is caught up in the same power discourse it seeks to counter. John criticizes the exploitative and luxurious Roman economy, and yet he clothes Jesus with its products and dreams of a golden city; John denounces violence against Christians, and yet he delights in violent bloody judgments.[57] Divine rule replicates Roman rule,[58] Christian formation mimics Imperial ethos,[59] and gender representation perpetuates misogynistic cultural understandings.[60] In the following, I shall present, in chronological order, the main representatives of this version of Revelation. They all share a deep commitment to different versions of post-structuralism.

Tina Pippin first theorized the misogynistic and imperialistic nature of Revelation by focusing on the pervasive gendered imagery of Revelation and by analyzing the political imperial dynamics informing Revelation's symbolic world.[61] Although Pippin claims to deploy a feminist/materialist lens, the material aspect is not fully covered. Pippin's main argument is that women in Revelation are always objects of male desire, not real women, but products of a chauvinistic imagination. Women are either dependent on men (the Bride, the woman clothed with the sun) and consequently proposed as positive characters, or they lack male controllers (Babylon, Jezebel) and thus are punished for their freedom. Babylon, in Pippin's interpretation, bears the traits of the whore in the Hebrew Bible in which prostitutes are either seen as heroines (Tamar in Gen 38 and Rahab in Jos 2 and 6) or as dangerous outcasts. Owner of her own sexuality and unapologetically in charge, Babylon poses a threat (to men) that "will not be tolerated."[62] Revelation's script erases any emancipatory trait by banishing all the women for, in the end, even the Bride "is replaced by the imagery of the city."[63]

Pippin, attentive to the ideological consequences of the literary devices, focuses on Babylon's demise in 17:16 and draws the consequence for the contemporary reader: Revelation's critique of Empire through the gendered image of Babylon evinces the hatred of women, the most misogynistic vision in the New Testament.[64] Such gender ideology, if left uncontested, has catastrophic consequences for our present as the authoritative nature of the text continues to haunt women's lives. The role of the reader ought to be oppositional; otherwise she is likely to become part of a history of oppression on women.[65]

If "Revelation against Empire" has been most thoroughly theorized by Schüssler Fiorenza, "Revelation complicit with Empire" has, in Stephen D. Moore, not only its most convincing defendant, but also its most comprehensive theorist. Schüssler Fiorenza's and Moore's oppositional evaluation of Revelation is not due to exegetical disagreements as much to their theoretical alignments and philosophical stances on meaning, agency, and the role of interpretation and Scripture. Revelation's divinity for Moore embodies the ultimate Imperial figure, a muscular bodybuilder sitting on a throne and occupying an iconic space somewhere in between Conan the Barbarian and the Emperor with his courtly devotees,[66] a God reenacting the imperial figure so closely that the one becomes undistinguishable from the other.[67] The Divine copies, both physically[68] and psychologically,[69] the features that define imperial authority.

Imperial replication starts with God as a new Emperor, but pervades every single aspect of Revelation itself. In fact, Moore's contribution to Revelation Studies can be interpreted as a progressive unveiling of Apocalypse's imperialistic agenda. Apocalyptic discourse, borrowing from Empire itself, defines community by way of othering in/outwards. Jezebel represents what ought to be expelled from the inside as much as Rome/Babylon exemplify what cannot enter from the outside. Deploying Bhabha's notion of mimicry, Moore understands John's discourse as a replica of what it seeks to keep at bay.[70] Similarly, turning to Judith Butler's theory of gender performance, Moore interprets the figure of Babylon as a sample of the most perfected imperial trope.[71] Roma is that "invincible warrior" "triumphantly enthroned upon the weapons of the armies she has vanquished."[72] Moore explores the Roman notion of *virtus* and, concluding it is basically a masculine value, asks the following question: "What, then, are we to make of Rhome/Roma, a female whose name is 'Strength', as we have seen, and who is the very emblem of masculine imperium? What does it mean that this is the image of imperial Rome that the provinces choose to reflect back to the metropolis? After rehearsing plausible interpretations to this conundrum (that is, how an armored woman can be the icon of a manly state), all of which points towards the instability of the image, Moore argues that that is precisely the weak point in the official representations that allows John to trash her. That is, John becomes aware of the potential inconsistencies in gender Roman ideology and uses them to his own purposes. If Roma is represented in Roman sources as a female with an inner masculine core, John shows that there is no 'masculine inner' core as such: All of it is purely degraded femininity. Revelation's attack on Roman Imperium is also an attack on Roman sex, done in Roman terms and thus, again, reinscribing language of imperium. For John, the problem lies in that Rome is not masculine enough.

Although the figure of the Lamb gestures towards a deconstruction of imperial dichotomies by blurring the distinction between masculine and feminine, animal and human, male and female, the language of Empire ends up "occupying" the Christian discourse. If Roma is the male imperium that constructs itself through an incessant suppression of femininity, Jesus is a celebration of masculinity that constructs itself likewise. Moore concludes: "Roman and John's Jesus are, to an extent, interchangeable figures,"[73] which explains, in advance, how Revelation was able to become the charter document of a different empire altogether, but an empire nonetheless.[74]

Christopher Frilingos reaches similar hermeneutical strategies and almost equal conclusions. Drawing on "gaze theory," the author explicitly introduces and situates Revelation as an expression of Roman culture. Such a methodological move is important because it no longer pits Christianity versus Empire, but situates Revelation at the center of imperial discourse. In addition it explicitly introduces a reflection on the nature of power as an inescapable phenomenon.[75] *Spectacles of Empire* foregrounds Revelation's appeal to ancient audiences by exploring the nature of the gaze (what it means "to look at") and concluding that Roman spectacles and Revelation share a dynamic in which spectators are not only subjects, but objects, of the gaze. The ones who look are the ones being "looked at." Being subjected to others' gaze has important consequences for gender roles in general, and for the consideration of the Lamb's masculinity in particular. In this view, the Lamb at once problematizes and reinforces hegemonic models of masculinity and appears as slain and slayer, pierced and piercer, penetrated and penetrator. Such destabilization should not lead interpreters to locate the "word" outside the "world," but rather at its very core. Although at times Revelation unsettles the hegemonic imperial gazing patterns, its message is best understood as an effect of the powers of the ancient spectacle – not only because it uses the very same dynamics, but because it draws readers into the same experience.

From this perspective, Frilingos interprets the demise of Babylon as a staged drama designed to seek disidentification from its audience. The spectators/readers are called to disidentify with the spectators of her demise who are portrayed in unmanly fashion. "Stripped and laid bare, the body of Babylon is not only foreign, exotic, and monstrous – it is also consumed." To suggest that this metaphor of destruction exclusively refers to the "laying waste" of a city and not to sexual violence, Frilingos concludes it to be oblivious that imperial ideology always operates at the sexual level and, consequently, "the conquest of Babylon remains at all times the rape of a prostitute."[76]

Besides Pippin, Moore, and Frilingos's monographs, there are other scholars who more closely deal with the figure of Babylon as an imperial trope. For instance, Stichele considers that it is not accidental that the targeted women (Jezebel and Babylon) lack male partners and thus control, and that the only males on the scene are presented as victims of these (voracious) women, deceived by them (2.20; 18.23).[77] It might seem that in Revelation, to use Thimmes's words, "the insider is a woman and the outsider is a man."[78] The Great Whore is consequently a literary device caught up in the controversies between competing masculinity models – the hegemonic one shaped by Empire and the minoritized one proposed by John.

Furthermore, when the issue of male representation of females is brought to bear on the analysis of Babylon, interpreters emphasize the phenomenon of stereotyping. The Great Whore is not, in the end, about women, but about men's fear of women. Following Pippin, Thimmes argues that the allure/wit of the Whore demands a male hero to survive or subdue her. The hero then, emerges, as a consequence of the control of the sexually deceptive, intellectually skilled, woman. Babylon's alluring power becomes even more powerful due to the vivid portrayal of her outer appearance. She is described in terms of vibrant colors and fragrant odors in clear distinction to the pure white garments of the New Jerusalem.[79] However, the utopian alternative does not, as Royalty argues, skip imperial wealth ideology as it mimics Roman values in a Christianized fashion.[80] Matthews brings together the economic and sexual consequences of Rome portrayed as a whore when he argues that John deploys the trope of the prostitute as an alluring figure that deceives men into all kinds of trades. Only when we adopt a view "from heaven," Revelation implies, are we able to see the prostitute as it really is: "filthy, greedy and disgusting."[81]

Most feminist or gender-critical approaches do not adhere to Schüssler Fiorenza's conclusions that Babylon should not be exclusively understood in gender terms. While acknowledging Schüssler Fiorenza's groundbreaking hermeneutical methodology, most ideological interpretations disagree with her conclusions that Babylon represents no woman. The conflation of woman and Empire leads these scholars to understand the ways in which political and gender aspects of the metaphor come together. Jean Kim summarizes the intersection when she argues that Babylon is not only the "other" as a woman, but also the other in terms of a land that needs to be conquered/destroyed. The rhetoric thus presumes and affirms an analogy between military and sexual invasion: the colonizer presented as male, the colonized as female.[82]

The authors introduced in this section, unanimously adopting literary criticism in post-structuralist fashion, also share a more or less developed concern for the contemporary political/ethical effects of "Revelatory ethics." It is precisely this concern that allows them to pay attention to the sexualized nature of the Babylon trope. On the one hand, the overall evaluation of the Apocalypse as a document that plays in the hand of Empire draws on many of Yarbro Collins's exegetical insights (mostly her theory than Revelation replicates the imperial gender system), but they depart from her "traditional" conception of language. On the other hand, Pippin, Moore, and Frilingos sympathize with Schüssler Fiorenza's project of attending to textual rhetorical effects in the present, but dismiss her overall evaluation as "naïve" for not paying sufficient attention to the implications of imperial sexual ethics.

Recapitulating: the Great Whore as imperial metaphor

To dismiss Revelation's violent imagery as anti-Christian, as politically ineffective in the present,[83] as playing into the hands of Empire,[84] as inspiration for an ethics of global resistance,[85] or as a template for religious activism,[86] rings true in the present only once the reality of the present Empire has been theorized. Furthermore, the ethical evaluation of the metaphor of the Great Whore needs to account for the sexualized nature of its meaning. Interpretations concerned with the ethical impact of Revelation, and more specifically with the deployment of Babylon/the Great Whore as an anti-imperial trope, pay great attention to strategies of resistance against the Roman Empire as well as to the ideological effects of using imperial methods. Most approaches that conceive of Revelation as resistant literature emphasize the difficult conditions under which first-century Christians had to negotiate their identity. On the other side, approaches that underline the complicit nature of Revelation with imperial politics stress that the book's ideology deploys imperial motifs and consequently is unable to escape the traps of Empire.

Both positions seek to update such ethical assessments by way of extrapolating John's strategies against Empire to the present. The figure of the Great Whore is understood as an anti-imperial trope transcending gender categories deployed by a minority group with important economic and political consequences or as an imperial image that "contaminates" Christian discourse with the gender ideology of Imperium. In both cases, critics pursue a thorough contextualization of Revelation within the Roman imperial system, but the reality of the present Empire as the venue where the actualization is to take place is completely missing. Both strategies offer a thoroughly contextualized understanding of Revelation in the past, which is then brought to bear on the reality of Empire in the present.[87] However, the reality of Empire is undertheorized.

At a general level, the evaluation of Revelation as resistant literature for the present does not adequately reflect the contemporary situation of Empire. In the following chapters, I argue that any ethical and political assessment of Revelation's relationship to Empire needs to incorporate a proper contextualization of the present. This is a pressing concern in contextual theologies and philosophies that, I contend, has not been properly translated into the hermeneutical task of interpreting the biblical text. What does it mean, after all, to think of Revelation as an anti or pro-imperial document if there is no historiographical model in place that grants a proper connection between the ethics of the past and the ethics of the present? Whereas ideological approaches rightly accuse historical-critical, socio-scientific, and narrative methodologies of betraying half a century of investigations on the hermeneutical circle, meaning-making, and interpreter's agency and contextualization, it is also the case that ideological criticism and its cognate cultural studies, with some notable exceptions, seem marooned by the idea of the unicity of meaning that needs to be teased from a text regardless of who interprets it. Regarding Revelation, this gridlock seems to have recently started to be cracked by approaches that situate at the center of the process of meaning-making the appropriation of meaning by specific communities, both in the past and in the present. Huber, for instance, has recently shifted her approach from an exclusively literary perspective to a cultural studies approach attentive to how different communities across time and space have re-appropriated Revelation's imagery for diverse political, ethical, and spiritual purposes. One of the goals of *Thinking and Seeing with Women in Revelation* is to study intercontextually, following John's injunction to "see," how Revelation's textual metaphoricity is taken in unexpected directions that, in turn, are pitted against the directions that the book itself takes. Particularly, Huber's feminist agenda proposes the role of past texts (Revelation) and its subsequent interpretations (visual and textual) as the hermeneutical places of community experience.[88]

Jacqueline Hidalgo and Lynne St. Clair Darden propose scripturalization as an approach that conceives of the act of interpretation as generative of life and death, as creating community, and as propelling communities into utopian futures. Hidalgo, on the one hand, takes the Chicanx experience as her starting point to lay out a minoritized ethnography of meaning production. Scripturalizing thus refers to the process of making meaning in the broadest political and cultural sense, the reconstruction of scriptures "not only to imagine themselves [people] and the places in which they live, but also make and remake scriptures as places to inhabit."[89] The inhabiting aspect of such process is especially relevant when the communities involved in the process have no place and conceive of scripture as home, of scripturalization as a homing devices. Hidalgo's contribution is groundbreaking in that it is inter-contextual through and through, conceiving of biblical texts as mediators of identities and thus dissolving the dichotomies of texts as objects and interpreters as subjects, of exegesis and hermeneutics, of communities in the past and communities in the present.[90]

Similarly, Lynne St. Clair Darden approaches Revelation from the perspective of scripturalization as a carrier of cultural memory, especially of the African American experience. Darden's understanding of the process differs from Hidalgo's in context (African-American diaspora vs. Chicanx) and emphasis (utopia oriented vs. cultural memory), but shares the same hermeneutical assumptions and ideological interests because it allows "for the simultaneous looking (and talking) back while moving forward, reshaping identity construction and in so doing reshaping the discipline itself."[91] My approach shares this overall concern of scripturalization meaning-making and seeks to explore the ways in which meaning travels and is remade in the process of its appropriation, especially, at a more theo-philosophical level, in the process of subject formation and desire-making. Unlike Hidalgo and Clair Darden, however, there is no experiential or specific cultural background that drives the hermeneutic process of making sense of Revelation 17–18, but rather, theoretical and historiographical preoccupations with the quandaries and entanglements of queer desire and imperial desire.

Notes

1 For a history of interpretation of Revelation, see Arthur William Wainwright, *Mysterious Apocalypse: Interpreting the Book of Revelation* (Nashville: Abingdon Press, 1993).

2 My project fully ascribes to the ethical turn. Elisabeth Schüssler Fiorenza first theorized this shift. She defines the "rhetorical-ethical approach," first in opposition to the supposedly objectivist, universalist, value-free paradigm that evaluates texts as windows providing historical information and, second, as form of enquiry that interprets texts for their impact on the audience, and their effects when readers submit to their worldviews; Elisabeth Schüssler Fiorenza, *Rhetoric and Ethic: The Politics of Biblical Studies* (Minneapolis, MN: Fortress Press, 1999). The scholarship that could be considered within the "ethical turn" has grown exponentially within the last two decades, incorporating all kinds of theories, methods, and optics. In the present study, I place special emphasis on Postcolonial and Queer Theories for their respective focus on identity as it emerges

from the relationship between Empires/Colonies in the first case, and Normalcy/Deviancy in the second.

3 Carter has suggested a fivefold approach: survival, accommodation, protest, dissent, and imitation. See Warren Carter, *The Roman Empire and the New Testament: An Essential Guide*, Abingdon Essential Guides (Nashville: Abingdon Press, 2006), 14–26. See also *John and Empire: Initial Explorations* (New York: T & T Clark, 2008), Chapter 2; Philip A. Harland, "Honouring the Emperor or Assailing the Beast: Participation in Civic Life among Associations (Jewish, Christian and Other) in Asia Minor and the Apocalypse of John," *Journal for the Study of the New Testament* no. 77 (2000).

4 Most notably, Boesak – anticipating Schüssler Fiorenza's stance – interprets Revelation as giving the reader a series of stark choices: obedience to God or subjection to Caesar, the Messiah or the Beast, New Jerusalem or Babylon. Boesak, writing with the reality of Apartheid in mind, parallels the persecution of South-African blacks with that of Jewish-Christians. Emphasizing its prophetic character, Boesak's Revelation is a call for action against the marginalizing structures of the national regime. See Allan Aubrey Boesak, *Comfort and Protest: Reflections on the Apocalypse of John of Patmos*, 1st ed. (Philadelphia: Westminster Press, 1987); Pablo Richard, *Apocalypse: A People's Commentary on the Book of Revelation*, The Bible & Liberation Series (Maryknoll: Orbis Books, 1995). In similar fashion, Richard sees Revelation as an opportunity to read the present from the perspective of the downtrodden, and makes the argument that Revelation is a book of conscientization. Revelation does not concern itself with the future but with the creation of an alternative present. Apocalypse is a resistance book that propels Christians to resist in the present; ibid.

5 Ricardo Foulkes, *El Apocalipsis De San Juan: Una Lectura Desde AméRica Latina* (Buenos Aires; Grand Rapids, MI: Nueva Creación; W. B. Eerdmans, 1989); Allen Dwight Callahan, "Babylon Boycott: The Book of Revelation," *Interpretation* 63, no. 1 (2009).

6 Adela Yarbro Collins, *Crisis and Catharsis: The Power of the Apocalypse*, 1st ed. (Philadelphia: Westminster Press, 1984). She makes the following influential clarification: "Relative, not absolute or objective, deprivation is a common precondition of millenarian movements. In other words, the crucial element is not so much whether one is actually oppressed as whether one feels oppressed," ibid., 84.

7 This same approach can be seen in Steven J. Friesen, *Imperial Cults and the Apocalypse of John: Reading Revelation in the Ruins* (Oxford; New York: Oxford University Press, 2001). More recently "Injustice or God's Will: Explanations of Poverty in Proto-Christian Texts," in *Christian Origins: People's History of Christianity*, ed. Richard A. Horsley (Minneapolis, MN: Fortress Press, 2005).

8 Warren Carter, "Accomodating 'Jezebel' and Withdrawing John: Negotiating Empire in Revelation Then and Now," *Interpretation* 63, no. 1 (2009). Other works who take the "inner controversy" as an hermeneutical key in reading Revelation and Empire: Leonard L. Thompson, *The Book of Revelation: Apocalypse and Empire* (New York: Oxford University Press, 1990); Robert M. Royalty, *The Streets of Heaven: The Ideology of Wealth in the Apocalypse of John* (Macon: Mercer University Press, 1998); Harry O. Maier, "Staging the Gaze: Early Christian Apocalypses and Narrative Self-Representation," *Harvard Theological Review* 90, no. 2 (1997).

9 Carter, "Accomodating 'Jezebel' and Withdrawing John: Negotiating Empire in Revelation Then and Now," 46. Carter nuances an oppositional approach to

both Empire/Revelation and Jezebel/John by highlighting the ways John rein-scribes imperial discursive practices.

10 For Yarbro Collins, the Apocalypse is the literary product of a conflict between a specific understanding of the Christian faith and a perceived crisis. A conflict triggered by a new set of expectations based on a religious system based on Jesus as Messiah; Yarbro Collins, *Crisis and Catharsis*, 106.

11 Ibid., 111–40.

12 Ibid., 134.

13 Yarbro Collins, *Crisis and Catharsis*, 138.

14 Ibid., 141.

15 Ibid., 152.

16 Yarbro Collins considers that "the solution of the Apocalypse is an act of crea-tive imagination which, like that of the schizophrenic, withdraws from empirical reality, from real experience in the everyday world," ibid., 155. In terms of its political effectiveness she considers that it keeps alive the utopia where political action is not feasible, ibid., 156.

17 "From a social-psychological viewpoint, the vision of a heavenly reality and of a radically new future functions as compensation for the relatively disadvan-taged situation of the hearers or as an imaginative way of resolving the tension between expectations and social reality," ibid., 154.

18 Ibid., 116.

19 Ibid., 123.

20 The political dimension of the combat myth relies in its ability to reinforce resist-ance and inspire martyrdom. It achieves these goals by imagining a victorious resolution of the conflict by way of destroying the readers' enemies; *The Combat Myth in the Book of Revelation*, Harvard Dissertations in Religion (Missoula, MT: Published by Scholars Press for Harvard theological review, 1976), 234.

21 *Crisis and Catharsis: The Power of the Apocalypse*, 160.

22 Ibid., 130.

23 As she argues, "The Jungian perspective leads us to find in the representation of Rome as the Great Mother a reflection of the struggle of Christian faith as a religion of individuation and consciousness to free itself from the Greco-Roman culture and religion, which were more rooted in the participation mystique," "Feminine Symbolism in the Book of Revelation," *Biblical Interpretation* 1, no. 1 (1993): 28.

24 "Women's History and the Book of Revelation," in *Society of Biblical Literature 1987 Seminar Papers*, ed. Kent Harold Richards (Atlanta, GA: Scholars Press, 1987), 91.

25 *Crisis and Catharsis: The Power of the Apocalypse*, 161.

26 Ibid., 166.

27 Ibid., 167.

28 Yarbro Collins concludes that "The dualist division of humanity in the Apoca-lypse is a failure in love (. . .) This dualism is destructive and dehumanizing (. . .) The act of denying others their full humanity diminishes the actor's humanity as well," ibid., 170.

29 "Feminine Symbolism in the Book of Revelation," 130.

30 Friesen, *Imperial Cults and the Apocalypse of John: Reading Revelation in the Ruins*, 140.

31 Three broad historical features determine John's response to the imperial structures:

1) The imperial cult became an increasingly totalitarian reality under Domitian.
2) Heightened unease regarding Jewish practices.
3) A pattern of escalating accommodation to Empire on behalf of the Christian communities.

32 Elisabeth Schüssler Fiorenza, *The Book of Revelation: Justice and Judgment*, 2nd ed. (Minneapolis, MN: Fortress Press, 1998), 6. The author conceives of Revelation as a utopia, "A world free of evil and suffering in order to give hope to those who are suffering and oppressed because they will not acknowledge the death-dealing political powers of their time," ibid., 25.

33 "It is therefore not femininity and sexual morality but the politics of power that is central to the argument of Revelation," in *The Power of the Word: Scripture and the Rhetoric of Empire* (Minneapolis, MN: Fortress Press, 2007), 135.

34 Ibid., 142.

35 *Democratizing Biblical Studies: Toward an Emancipatory Educational Space*, 1st ed. (Louisville: Westminster John Knox Press, 2009), 112.

36 *Sharing Her Word: Feminist Biblical Interpretation in Context* (Boston: Beacon Press, 1998), 144.

37 *The Power of the Word: Scripture and the Rhetoric of Empire*, 145.

38 *The Book of Revelation: Justice and Judgment*, 199.

39 G. K. Beale, *Revelation: A Commentary on the Greek Text*, The New International Greek Testament Commentary (Grand Rapids: W.B. Eerdmans, 1998).

40 Ibid., 3.

41 Ibid., 33.

42 Ibid., 880–95. This emphasis on the cultic nature of the imperial critique shows especially when Beale offers comprehensive statements about the main rhetorical goals in the book; ibid., 885. A similar approach regarding Revelation's stance towards Empire can be found in the other monumental work on the Apocalypse: David Aune, following historical-critical approach, also relegates the oppositional stance of Revelation to the religious level and not the material conditions of exploitation or marginalization; David E. Aune, *Revelation 17–22* (Nashville: T. Nelson, 1998), 990.

43 Craig R. Koester, "Roman Slave Trade and the Critique of Babylon in Revelation 18," *The Catholic Biblical Quarterly* 70, no. 4 (2008).

44 Lynn R. Huber, *Like a Bride Adorned: Reading Metaphor in John's Apocalypse* (New York: T&T Clark International, 2007).

45 Ibid., 182.

46 Ibid., 73–5.

47 Barbara R. Rossing, *The Choice Between Two Cities: Whore, Bride, and Empire in the Apocalypse* (Harrisburg: Trinity Press International, 1999).

48 Ibid., 18.

49 Rossing, *The Choice Between Two Cities*, 158. The most pointed contrast between the political economies of New Jerusalem and Babylon is the disappearance of the "sea" in Rev 21:1 bringing about the demise of the shipping economy. See also the motif of water of life as a gift without price (Rev 21:6 and 22:17) vs. the deadly springs in Rev 16:4. Appeal to the audience's desire is made explicit with the verb *thelein* in Rev 22:17. The bride invokes the audience's desire for the water of life and all the gifts of New Jerusalem. For those who make the choice to follow the ethical path of faithfulness to God and rejection of Babylon, the bride represents the promise of a share in the New Jerusalem and an inheritance "in the tree of life and God's holy city" (Rev 22:19).

50 John W. Marshall, "Gender and Empire: Sexualized Violence in John's Anti-Imperial Apocalypse," in *A Feminist Companion to the Apocalypse of John*, ed. Amy-Jill Levine (London; New York: T&T Clark, 2009). Marshall draws upon Bhabha who in turn uses Fanon to illustrate the violent dynamic against Jezebel. Fanon writes: "The colonized man will first manifest this aggressiveness which has been deposited in his bones against his own people. This is the period when niggers beat each other up, and the police and the magistrates do not know which way to turn when faced with the astonishing waves of crime in

North Africa'; 'thus collective auto-destruction in a very concrete form is one of the ways in which the native's muscular tension is set free"; Frantz Fanon, *The Wretched of the Earth*, 1st Evergreen ed. (New York: Grove Weidenfeld, 1991), 52. John depicts a female character as the conduit of contamination between the insider community and the contaminating influence of the outside, the other. Jezebel broaches the border that ought not to be crossed.

51 Mark D. Mathews, *Riches, Poverty, and the Faithful: Perspectives on Wealth in the Second Temple Period and the Apocalypse of John*, Society for New Testament Studies Monograph Series (Cambridge: Cambridge University Press, 2013), 217. Notice here the parallelism with Schüssler Fiorenza's argument.

52 David M. Rhoads, *From Every People and Nation: The Book of Revelation in Intercultural Perspective* (Minneapolis, MN: Fortress Press, 2005), 4.

53 Brian K. Blount, "The Witness of Active Resistance: The Ethics of Revelation in African American Perspective," in *From Every People and Nation: The Book of Revelation in Intercultural Perspective*, ed. David M. Rhoads (Minneapolis, MN: Fortress Press, 2005), 45.

54 Justo L. González, "Revelation: Clarity and Ambivalence: A Hispanic/Cuban American Perspective," ibid.

55 Clarice Martin, "Polishing the Unclouded Mirror: A Womanist Reading of Revelation 18:13," ibid., 86.

56 It is interesting to note that Martin uses Leonard Thompson who advocates that Revelation is almost a paranoid document in that there is no historical evidence that Christians experienced any oppression.

57 Stephen D. Moore, *Empire and Apocalypse: Postcolonialism and the New Testament*, Bible in the Modern World V. 12 (Sheffield, UK: Sheffield Phoenix Press, 2006); *God's Gym : Divine Male Bodies of the Bible* (New York: Routledge, 1996).

58 Royalty, *The Streets of Heaven*.

59 On Imperial cults see: Christopher A. Frilingos, *Spectacles of Empire: Monsters, Martyrs, and the Book of Revelation*, Divinations (Philadelphia: University of Pennsylvania Press, 2004).

60 Moore, *Empire and Apocalypse: Postcolonialism and the New Testament*. For discussion see S. R. F. Price, *Rituals and Power: The Roman Imperial Cult in Asia Minor* (Cambridge; New York: Cambridge University Press, 1984); J. Nelson Kraybill, *Imperial Cult and Commerce in John's Apocalypse*, Journal for the Study of the New Testament Supplement Series (Sheffield, UK: Sheffield Academic Press, 1996).

61 Tina Pippin, "Eros and the End: Reading for Gender in the Apocalypse of John," *Semeia* no. 59 (1992).

62 *Death and Desire: The Rhetoric of Gender in the Apocalypse of John*, 1st ed. (Louisville: Westminster/John Knox Press, 1992); "Eros and the End: Reading for Gender in the Apocalypse of John"; "The Heroine and the Whore: Fantasy and the Female in the Apocalypse of John," in *From Every People and Nation: The Book of Revelation in Intercultural Perspective*, ed. David M. Rhoads ((Minneapolis, MN: Fortress Press, 2005).

63 "The Heroine and the Whore: Fantasy and the Female in the Apocalypse of John," 132.

64 Ibid., 138.

65 Ibid., 132.

66 Moore considers that the theology and ideology of Revelation represents the apotheosis of imperial ideology, "Its ascension to a transhistorical site"; Stephen D. Moore, "The Beatific Vision as a Posing Exhibition: Revelation's Hypermasculine Deity," *Journal for the Study of the New Testament* no. 60 (1995): 35.

67 "For in and through Revelation, the emperor ascends into heaven and becomes a god, and the god he becomes is none other than Yahweh. John's attempt to counter the magnificent imperial cult with the image of a yet more magnificent heavenly cult (the latter modeled in part upon the former) has resulted in a fascinating (con)fusion of figures, the Roman emperor coalescing with the Jewish-Christian God," ibid., 49.

68 A rainbow, just like the one Suetonius attributes to Domitian; ibid., 35.

69 God's glory, as that of the bodybuilder, is meaningless without a spectacle reminding him of his grandiose: "And that is precisely what the God of Revelation craves. Indeed, this vast audience of idolizers – nameless, faceless, countless (cf. 5.11–13; 7.9–10; 19.1–8) – is actually nothing more than an infinite row of mirrors lining the interior walls of the heavenly city, which turns out to be a perfect cube some 12,00 stadia (approximately 1500 miles) high, broad and long (21.16; cf. 1 Kgs 6.20). And the sole purpose of this vast mirrored enclosure is eternally to reflect the divine perfection back to the divinity himself. The emperor has become his own love object," ibid., 49.

70 Ibid., 51; "Questions of Biblical Ambivalence and Authority under a Tree Outside Delhi; or, the Postcolonial and the Postmodern," in *Postcolonial Biblical Criticism: Interdisciplinary Intersections*, eds. Stephen D. Moore and Fernando F. Segovia (London; New York: T & T Clark International, 2007).

71 "The Beatific Vision as a Posing Exhibition: Revelation's Hypermasculine Deity," 54.

72 "Metonymies of Empire: Sexual Humiliation and Gender Masquerade in the Book of Revelation," in *Postcolonial Interventions* (Sheffield, UK: Sheffield Phoenix Press, 2009), 77. See also "Questions of Biblical Ambivalence and Authority under a Tree Outside Delhi; or, the Postcolonial and the Postmodern,".

73 "Metonymies of Empire: Sexual Humiliation and Gender Masquerade in the Book of Revelation," 77.

74 More recently, Moore and Glancy argue that Babylon is portrayed as an interstitial figure between the *porne* and the *hetaira*: she has many sexual partners resembling the most degraded sexual worker (tattoos included). She sits on the throne and fucks with the kings of earth. Tacitus's Messalina suits the comparison here: the historical female is the overly sexual woman, paragon of imperial autocracy with no restraint, hungering for land, wealth and power. Jennifer A. Glancy and Stephen D. Moore, "How Typical a Roman Prostitute Is Revelation's 'Great Whore'?" *Journal of Biblical Literature* 130, no. 3 (2011): 555.

75 Frilingos, *Spectacles of Empire*.

76 Ibid., 106.

77 Caroline Vander Stichele, "Re-Membering the Whore: The Fate of Babylon According to Revelation 17.16," in *A Feminist Companion to the Apocalypse of John*, ed. Amy-Jill Levine (London; New York: T&T Clark, 2009).

78 Pamela Thimmes, " 'Teaching and Beguiling My Servants': The Letter to Thyatira (Rev. 2.18–29)," ibid.

79 As Carey puts it "Revelation characterizes Babylon as a decadent, sensually coded woman and the New Jerusalem as a modest virgin prepared for her wedding day,"; Greg Carey, "A Man's Choice: Wealth Imagery and the Two Cities of the Book of Revelation," ibid., 148.

80 Royalty, *The Streets of Heaven*, 245–6.

81 Mathews, *Riches, Poverty, and the Faithful*, 94.

82 Jean K Kim, " 'Uncovering Her Wickedness': An Inter(Con)Textual Reading of Revelation 17 from a Postcolonial Feminist Perspective," *Journal for the Study of the New Testament* 73 (1999): 73. Stichele further reminds the readers that Schüssler Fiorenza's approach is like watching a horror movie reminding oneself that it is just fake blood.

83 Yarbro Collins concludes that a Christian theology cannot afford to foster prayers for the destruction of one's enemies, because one runs the risk of becoming like the oppressor. Adela Yarbro Collins, "Persecution and Vengeance in the Book of Revelation," in *Apocalypticism in the Mediterranean World and the Near East* (Tübingen: Mohr Siebeck, 1983), 746–47.

84 J. Nelson Kraybill, *Apocalypse and Allegiance: Worship, Politics, and Devotion in the Book of Revelation* (Grand Rapids, MI: Brazos Press, 2010).

85 Michael J. Gorman, *Reading Revelation Responsibly: Uncivil Worship and Witness: Following the Lamb into the New Creation* (Eugene: Cascade Books, 2011).

86 Craig R. Koester, "Revelation's Visionary Challenge to Ordinary Empire," *Interpretation* 63, no. 1 (2009): 18.

87 Such diagnosis applies, in my view, to Empire Studies in the field of the New Testament. See Rossing, *The Choice Between Two Cities*, 164.

88 Lynn R. Huber, *Thinking and Seeing Women in Revelation* (London; New York: Bloomsbury, 2013).

89 Jacqueline M. Hidalgo, *Revelation in Aztlán: Scriptures, Utopias, and the Chicano Movement* (New York: Palgrave Macmillan, 2016), 17.

90 I consider intercontextual readings as those interpretations that focus on how different texts and their contexts merge together in the production of contemporary meanings; See Luis Menéndez-Antuña, "The Queer Art of Biblical Reading: Matthew 25:31–46 (*Caritas Christiana*) Through *Caritas Romana*," *Journal of Religious Ethics* 45, no. 4 (2017): 732–59.

91 Lynne St. Clair Darden, *Scripturalizing Revelation: An African American Postcolonial Reading of Empire* (Atlanta: Society of Biblical Literature, 2015), 33.

2 Thinking apocalyptic resistance in the age of empire

Introduction

Empire has been, as many political theorists acknowledge, one the most influential theorizations of the global order in the first quarter of twenty-first century.[1] Despite strong and firm disagreements raised from the left and blatant opposition from the right, *Empire* and its sequels[2] have contributed to frame the contemporary debate about the process of globalization and global capitalism and have presented a holistic view of resistance. Consequently, *Empire* is a privileged starting point to think about the contextualization of resistance in the present and to propose a comparative reading of subversive and resistant strategies as seen in Revelation and contemporary politics.[3] More specifically, *Empire* – as much as the literature produced in its aftermath[4] – provides a general framework by which to explore further bodily resistance to imperial formations in the present, with important consequences to read the past.

Although notably inspired by Marxist theory, Hardt and Negri draw upon postmodern thinking with the goal of deconstructing traditional binarisms and offering a new conceptual template to think about the effects of political economy on culture, society, and – the focus of this book – subjectivity. Traditional Marxist conceptions of power, they argue, fail to capture the multilayered nature of oppression and the changes in economic theory; they also fail to account for the process of subject formation typical of twenty-first-century capitalistic development. On these issues, *Empire* is an innovative theoretical piece that opens a space for new liberationist re-appropriations of Scripture situated within the ethical turn.

I take Hardt and Negri's contribution as a point of departure for several reasons. First, they provide us with a comprehensive account of the current global political economy. Second, their theorization of resistance attends to subject formation and incorporates the emancipatory potential of the body as site of resistance. Third, their theoretical framework, deeply indebted to Foucault, allows for a complementary approach to theories of global justice and bodily resistance. Fourth, their reliance on Foucault allows the historian to bridge a gap, still prominent in biblical interpretation, as diagnosed in Chapter 1, between the ethics of the past and its relevance to the present.[5]

Definition of empire

Hardt and Negri propose an idea of Empire as a new world order that succeeds the regime of Imperialism. They conceptualize the passage from Imperialism to Empire through the notion of the demise of the nation-state as the exclusive unit of political sovereign power: this shift is determined by change in the role of the nation-state, no longer the territorial hub for colonial expansion, but a looser political entity with a less tight sovereignty, that gives rise to a global order. This new order (Empire) is all-encompassing, incorporating "the entire global realm within its open, expanding frontiers. Empire manages hybrid identities, flexible hierarchies, and plural exchanges through modulating networks of command.[6] Such is the new face, Hardt and Negri argue, of contemporary global capitalism. Two traits define Empire: it has a totalizing scope and it has no center. The first characteristic, as I shall show, conceives Empire as a reality with no outside, whereas the second envisions it as a set of networks of power.

The supposed demise of the nation-state as the exclusive political entity that explains the relationship established by all kinds of imperialisms between metropolises and colonies demands a theoretical move that redefines power as a force with no center. In Imperialism, the nation-state symbolizes the center of domination in terms of military power and economic, political, and cultural dominance.[7] All of these traits remain, in singular form, in Empire but under new configurations. Whereas Imperialism "typically signifies the top rank of a hierarchy of powerful sovereign states in which power elites shape the grand strategies of the most important power projects, including imperial ones,"[8] in Empire we can no longer find the pyramid-like structure of power but a complex mesh of interlocking ties, a collection of networks in which power is concentrated at specific points.[9] The political power that resided in the nation-state has been disseminated over a wide variety of structures with no fixed center. In concrete terms, the United States – once representative of hegemonic political power – has assumed a transnational configuration.[10] Global governance is rooted now in a series of assemblages and authorities that together trigger an emerging imperial formation that is sustainable only through the interlocking collaboration of national, supranational, and non-national entities.[11]

The demise of the nation-state as a power hub calls for a reconceptualization of power itself, both in terms of analyzing its workings and proposing new venues of subversion and resistance. The result of the transnationalization and deterritorialization of a center is that "the unity of single governments has been disarticulated and invested in a series of separate bodies (banks, international organisms of planning, and so forth, in addition to the traditional separate bodies), which all increasingly refer for legitimacy to the transnational level of power."[12] Such power transference does not imply that the nation-state has been divested of its power, but rather that it is no longer the privileged category of analysis. The nation-state, powerful as it might be, becomes a virtual tool in the hands of transnational capital: a tool that implements the necessary policies that protect capital or the main beneficiary of its global operations. National capitalism with the United States as its main driving force has given rise to global capitalism.

The European Empires defined themselves in relationship to the Other; that is, they built up their identity by subjugating the Other. Global capitalism, however, has no Other and is all-encompassing. The US, Hardt and Negri continue, sits at the top of the pyramidal structure, a privileged position that is the historical result of its own constitutional history. The authors consider that, in this regard, the US is the legitimate heir of imperial Rome and its rule and that, as such, republican rule results from a synthesis of diverse forms of government (monarchic, aristocratic, and democratic power) brought together in equilibrium.[13] For Polybius, monarchy guarantees unity and continuity of power, aristocracy defines justice and virtue, and democracy organizes the demos so that the people can be ruled and the regime can be constrained. Similarly, the authors argue, Empire today maintains itself through a functional balance between three modes of power: first, the monarchic unity and its monopoly of force; second, transnational corporations governed by aristocracies; and third, the democratic dimensions present in nation-states and other popular organisms.[14]

The focus here should be on the third tier of command in Empire, which is the broadest and is made up of groups invested in popular representation and communication, including mass media, global forums, cultural industries, and NGOs. Empire then is shaped through its "hybrid constitution" with its monarchic, aristocratic, and democratic functions merging inextricably. Empire is "born through the global expansion of the internal US constitutional project,"[15] whose military mobilization must articulate a series of international institutions that have political, economic, and cultural control.

Political resistance in this global order takes numerous shapes. Here, I am mostly interested in the resistance that can be found in the body conceived of as a tool, as relational knot with the potential to resist Empire's machine. In order to explore how the body can exert resistance, I will show how Hardt and Negri take their cue from Michael Foucault and expand the idea that "where there is power there is resistance" to address the question of the production of subjectivities within the realm of biopower. Subjectivity is the space carved out by power and, consequently, the place where new resistant strategies can take place. Foucault's analysis of biopower, they argue, has the potential to go beyond the description of the anatomy of power into the formulation or imagination of new forms of subjectivity.[16] Such new forms, however, call for imaginative productive ways of configuring bodies, minds, and souls that run against, paradoxically enough, the inclusive nature of Empire. The traditional boundaries of race, creed, color, gender, sexual orientation, and so on are collapsing under the umbrella of Empire, taking away the subversive potential of the constituent subjectivities with the result that "a smooth space across which subjectivities glide without substantial resistance or conflict" is created.[17]

Empire and the body: bodily resistance

Power dispersion does not operate exclusively at the macropolitical level, but causes a change at the level of local institutions that have decisive power over the subject. Hardt and Negri draw on Foucault to portray the passage from disciplinary to control societies. Power traditionally allocated in disciplinary institutions such as schools and medical and legal organizations has spread and become integrated into every microaspect of everyday life. The purpose of power is no longer to discipline but to create and control a wide new range of subjectivities that no longer fit in the straitjacket of identities that was typical in the disciplinary society.[18]

The transition to a control society also brings about a shift from transcendent to immanent power. In the control society, there is an intensification of the normalizing apparatuses that extends beyond them to reach the subjects in their own regulation.[19] The society of control exerts biopower as a kind of power that regulates life from its interior, regulating it and producing it.[20] Power now is expressed "as a control that extends throughout the depths of the consciousness and bodies of the population – and at the same time across the entirety of social relations."[21] From this standpoint, biopower serves the purpose of expansive global capitalism by helping it to produce both commodities and subjectivities. Through biopower, capitalism has extended its arms from the production of goods to the production of subjectivities and identities.

Global capitalism does bring about a society of control characterized by "an intensification and generalization of the normalizing apparatuses of disciplinarity that internally animate our common and daily practices, but in contrast to discipline, this control extends well outside the structured sites of social institutions through flexible and fluctuating networks."[22] The blurring of the dichotomy inside/outside that characterizes Empire also affects the way institutions shape subjectivity. For one, subjectivities are produced in the social factory, that is, they are shaped according to the needs, demands, and impositions of discrete institutions. But more important, as far as the production of subjectivity goes, the transition from Imperialism to Empire results in discrete institutions no longer exclusively affecting discrete spaces but spilling over a whole range of areas and conditions: we are always in the family, in the school, in the prison, in the hospital.[23] Or, as the authors put it, "the imperial society of control is tendentially everywhere the order of the day."[24]

Although I shall dwell on resistance further below, this analysis poses the question of the place of counter-action at the heart of Empire. If control is everywhere, one might ask, how can we think about an emergent resistant subjectivity? Hardt and Negri identify a virtual point for resistance at the juncture of the political and economic subject. The paradox results from the fact that the networks of control rule each subjectivity but at the same time the networks require an autonomous subject able to produce and consume.

One obstacle to the resolution of an actively resistant subjectivity is that we live in the society of the spectacle, where media manipulation dictates what exists and how we think of it. Submissive subjectivities are possible because spectacle functions through fear, although under the appearance of desire and pleasure.[25]

Despite their reliance on Foucault's theory of power to analyze the shift from Imperialism to Empire, Hardt and Negri pay little attention to the body as a network of power itself, one that is thus equipped to exert resistance. Yet they hint at the necessity of thinking anew of the body as site for resistance. The condition of possibility for a mutated/posthuman body is the continuity between human nature and nature itself: there are no clear-cut distinctions between the human and the animal, the human and the machine, male and female, and so on. They define contemporary experiments on the body as an "anthropological exodus" with the potential to operate against Empire. The resistant body, unwilling to submit, must be a body that "is incapable of adapting to family life, to factory discipline, to the regulations of a traditional sex life, and so forth."[26] This body has to be able to create new life, which, in Hardt and Negri's mind, resembles the Spinozian project of a body product of high consciousness and infused with love. Such is, in their view, a re-conceptualization of the domesticized body in the age of Empire. Particularly helpful for my purpose, apart from the acknowledgment of the need to keep working on bodily hybridity, is the location of subversive strategies under the notion of anthropological exodus conceived of as a migration to a non-place within the possibilities already available under Empire.

Despite their novel insights, the authors do not theorize what the project of conceiving the body as migrating to a non-place might look like. In the following, I seek to fill in the gaps left in such theorization through the work of Foucault on the Greek and Roman body. My goal is twofold: first, to show how Foucault's historiography is able to bridge the gap between the present and the past thus helping in a reconstruction of the politics of bodily resistance in the Book of Revelation for the present; second, to explore how situating such theorization within the context of the present Empire contributes to the project, largely undertheorized in Foucault, of relating bodily resistance to imperial economy.

Foucault, knowledge, power, and the subject

Foucault's philosophical project can be understood broadly as a reflection on the processes of subject formation, or of how "human beings are made subject."[27] The study of subjectivity or how subject formation occurs is deeply related to the question of governability, for the subject is formed by regimes of power. However, as is well known in Foucauldian studies, the power that shapes the subject is not conceived of as coming "from above," or "from outside." Instead, being a subject means being subjected and exercising subjectivity.

This notion of power runs contrary to Marxist notions that tend to theorize power relations as coming "from a center and from above."[28] In contrast, Foucault talks about disciplinary power as a mechanism that regulates behavior through complex systems of surveillance that do not affect the body but create it. Power is no longer an external force that affects an already existent materiality, but a network of forces that shape bodily existence from the outset. Discipline concerns itself with producing docile, healthy, productive bodies that can be put to work, and thus can commit themselves to the progression of the capitalist system.[29] Schools, medical institutions, universities, and job etiquettes are all part of a cultural network that seeks to discipline the subject into individuality. The ultimate effect is to create a "docile body." There is no longer need for specific forms of physical coercion since the disciplinary regimes have created a body that abides by the systems' requirements.

Foucault's analyses hinge on an innovative conception of power/resistance. In an often-quoted passage, Foucault writes:

> Where there is power, there is resistance, and yet, or rather consequently, this resistance is never in a position of exteriority in relation to power. Should it be said that one is always "inside" power, there is no "escaping" it, there is no absolute outside where it is concerned, because one is subject to the law in any case? (. . .) This would be to misunderstand the strictly relational character of power relationships. Their existence depends on a multiplicity of points of resistance: these play the role of adversary, target, support, or handle in power relations. These points of resistance are present everywhere in the power network. Hence there is no single locus of great refusal, no soul of revolt, source of all rebellions, or pure law of the revolutionary.[30]

Such a conception of power locates resistance at the center of power, not at the margins of it. This has important consequences because it means that resistance's effectiveness or success ought to be evaluated in specific contexts. Such evaluation needs to take into consideration how different networks of power that manifest themselves through a wide variety of institutions interact, allow, or occlude equally diffuse networks of resistance.

Two insights are particularly important for my project of thinking bodily resistance: resistance always takes place in an ambiguous space, and power and resistance need not be located at opposite ends of the same spectrum. In the same way, as Hardt and Negri argued, Empire is an all-encompassing reality in which resistance is possible when the multitude operates and benefits from the waves of power. Bodily resistance is possible through the mechanisms that have constituted the subject as such. Furthermore, resistance does not need to talk back to power on its own terms: the relationship between power and resistance need not be bi-directional. Resistance is related to the discovery and reenactment of subjugated knowledges and to the discovery of their relationship to hegemonic/oppressive discourses. By "subjugated knowledges" Foucault means two different but related things: on the one hand, he refers to historical contents that were available at specific points of history but were buried, masked, or occluded and are now being retrieved through the tools of scholarship;[31] on the other, he refers to a series of knowledges "that have been disqualified as nonconceptual knowledges, as insufficiently elaborated knowledges: naïve knowledges, hierarchically inferior knowledges (. . .) the knowledge of the delinquent."[32]

The fight among knowledges (in the plural) is not along the axis of truth/ cognition but along the axis of power effects.[33] Genealogically speaking, competing discourses should not be analyzed or evaluated in terms of the relationship between claim and fact, but in terms of their power effects. Because knowledge is deeply situated, the power effects of the discourse invariably change showing that "what looks like right, law, or obligation from the point of view of power looks like the abuse of power, violence, and exaction when it is seen from the viewpoint of the new discourse."[34] This relationship between power and knowledge informs a genealogical approach to the historical archive in particular, and to the task of the historian in general. In the fourth lecture delivered on 28 January 1976, Foucault sets out to provide some methodological keys to write a counter-history of race. He starts by signaling how historical discourse has been traditionally linked "to the rituals of power."[35] The labor of the historian he sees as a justification and a reinforcement of the hegemonic power, which, Foucault continues, has two important power effects: it binds together and it immobilizes. This "Jupiterian" history is the "discourse of power, the discourse of the obligations power uses to subjugate; it is also the dazzling discourse that power uses to fascinate, terrorize, and immobilize."[36]

History, far from being an objective accounting of historical facts, plays into the hand of hegemonic knowledge by providing legitimizing support in that it perpetuates the power dynamics among social interactions. Foucault goes on to say that "the point of recounting history, the history of kings, the mighty sovereigns and their victories (and, if need be, their temporary defeats) was to use the continuity of the law to establish a juridical link between those men and power, because power and its workings were a demonstration of the continuity of the law itself. History's other role was to use the almost unbearable intensity of the glory of power, its examples and its exploits, to fascinate men."[37] The unearthing of under-histories counteracts discourses of unity and purity[38] by complicating the relationships between power and resistance. To put it differently, resistance needs to be thought of as more than the "antimatter of power." For Foucault, there cannot be a totalizing view of resistance because that would bring about a totalitarian regime. Resistance, Foucault also suggests, lies in the way a subject fashions herself in order to create and pursue the aesthetic experience that departs from contemporary modes of subjectification. He suggests that one's life should be lived out as an art form rather than by conforming to a set of juridical forms or an attested nature. A self that works on an aesthetic of the self aims to configure a space in which the self can imagine relationships anew. The project of "inventing" new subjectivities sits at the heart of Foucault's study of antiquity.

Classical subjectivity

Foucault's focus on classical Greece and late antiquity is a genealogical project of discovering ways of understanding subjectivity that can resist contemporary regimes of the normal. Foucault's philosophy is a way to "promote new forms of subjectivity through the refusal of this kind of individuality which has been imposed on us for several centuries."[39] Foucault blames Christianity for having imposed on us a conception of the self that depends on confessional practices to come into being, and for its contribution to the erasure of an "aesthetics of the self" that conceived of ethics not so much as a set of abstract principles but as a way to relate to the self in creative ways. This particular genealogical project is thus an invitation to understand the subject beyond the inherited traditions of the "Christian self." Christianity, although sharing a common understanding with the Greeks about austerity, shifted the focus towards a "hermeneutics of desire" concerned with telling the truth about oneself. Whereas for the Greeks ethics was concerned with fashioning the self as a work of art, Christianity inaugurated the field of ethics as a set of rules to which the subject needs to conform. Christianity, continues Foucault, dissociates pleasure from desire, problematizing desire as the mark of a fallen humanity.[40]

Greek ethics of the self

A deep ethical concern for the present drives Foucault's study of Greek and Roman cultures, for he sees in classical subjectivity a counter-balance to the moralization of sex that Christianity brought about and that, later on in the nineteenth century, informed the arrival of "sexuality" as a disciplinary project. The Greek configuration of subjectivity around the notion of *chresis aphrodision* as an art of oneself in which the self works on oneself is a starting point from which to consider alternative ways of thinking about selfhood and, more crucially, to start imagining new shapes for the contours of ethics as a discipline.

Foucault distinguishes three meanings in the concept of morality: the moral code, the way individuals behave, and, most important, the ways in which the subject submits or modifies herself to conform to or to contest the moral code.[41] Foucault focuses on the third item because of his interest in subjectification. Furthermore, there are four areas that need to be studied in historical ethics: substance, the mode of subjection, the techniques of the self, and the telos.

The ethical substance is the material that provides "matter for reflection." In *On the Genealogy of Ethics*, Foucault explains:

> For the Greeks, when a philosopher was in love with a boy, but did not touch him, his behavior was valued. The problem was: Does he touch the boy or not? That's the ethical substance: the act linked with pleasure and desire. For Augustine (. . .) what bothers him is what exactly was the kind of desire he had for him (his friend.)[42]

The mode of subjectification refers to the ways in which moral obligations are enforced or seen as legitimate. The third aspect concerns the agency of the subject:

> what are we to do, either to moderate our acts, or to decipher what we are, or to eradicate our desires, or to use our sexual desire in order to obtain certain aims (. . .) ascetism in a very broad sense.[43]

The telos, the fourth aspect, refers to the aspirations of the moral path. "For instance, shall we become pure, or immortal, or free, or masters of ourselves, and so on?"[44]

The core of classical ethics was not so much that there are forbidden/ permitted acts but rather how to handle them.[45] Foucault coins the term "aesthetics of existence" to explore how the Greek male citizen was not concerned with abiding by a set of abstract principles but with stylizing his practice in order to accomplish mastery over his pleasures. Mastery of the self is the "power which one exercises over oneself through the power which one exercises over others. *Enkrateia*, or the mastery of oneself, was the condition of possibility to master others."[46] Accordingly, classical ethics conceives of ethics as a work of art, as the creative task of laboring on one-self to achieve beauty. Ethics is a way of forming oneself, of achieving one's best by working on its improvement. What interests Foucault here is not so much the art itself as the general trajectory that one can discern in moral judgment: ethics is not so much about acts as it is about creation. It is also a creation that goes beyond personal ethics because it is closely tied to the ethics of the polis: domination of the self is the requirement for domination of the other, mastery of the polis demands mastery of the self. There is a continuum between "sexual virility," "social virility," and "ethical virility," or, as O'Leary puts it, "between sexual mastery, social mastery, and ethical self-mastery."[47]

John Winkler, among many others, points out how "maleness" was not a given but an achievement that was always endangered,[48] thus the need to be vigilant over attitudes that would endanger one's masculinity. From this perspective, to be penetrated equals losing control over oneself and, conse-quently, being unable to control others. To say it with Elisabeth Schüssler

Fiorenza, to be at the top of the kyriarchy means, literally, to be on top. As Foucault further notes:

> To form oneself as a virtuous and moderate subject in the use he makes of pleasures, the individual has to construct a relationship with the self that is of the "domination-submission," "command-obedience," "mastery-docility" type (and not, as will be the case in Christian spirituality, a relationship of the "elucidation-renunciation," "decipherment-purification" type). This is what could be called the "heautocratic" structure of the subject in the ethical practice of the pleasures.[49]

This style of ethics continues in the Imperial period with important changes. Foucault titles volume III "Care of the Self" to signal a shift in focus from an ethics focused on working on the beauty of oneself to an ethics that is concerned with proper enjoyment. Stoicism, Foucault argues, focuses on the desire to become an object of pleasure oneself,[50] but not as a pleasure that comes from the outside but as one acquired through self-possession. *Aphrodisia* remains the substance that needs to be combated; yet this time, because the individual is weaker, one needs to invent a new set of rules and techniques to strengthen oneself. At the same time, the requirement to become subject to a certain way of living is universalized because stoicism depends on the idea of natural universal law. Self-control, scrutiny, and abstinence acquire importance for, at the level of telos, self-mastery remains central. Such a relationship of oneself to the self is similar to that of a judge but in a way that skips modernist notions of the judicial system. Foucault uses the metaphor of the inspector who evaluates a piece of work to counteract the idea of a judge who would look for "infractions," and whose would be to determine a final verdict.[51]

The culture of the self

For Imperial Roman culture, *Aphrodisia* remains the subject of sexual ethics, and is typically theorized as a force that needs to be contained. Foucault argues that Roman culture has a weaker conception of the self/subject than Greek culture. Roman thinkers also introduce universal principles that derive from nature and reason and that apply to everyone regardless of social status. Such "democratization" calls for techniques of abstinence and self-control that keep the goal of self-mastery in place. There is an emphasis now on the pleasure of self-possession that derives from the difficulty of mastering the weak self. The weaker understanding of the self, the introduction of universal law, and the emphasis of self-mastery impose new structures on the marital institution and on the relationship with boys. What is particularly interesting and novel in Foucault's approach is that the shift was not so much triggered by a change in the code of ethics but was the outcome of a change in the form of ethical subjectivation. That is, the relation of the self to others changed as a result of important changes in political structures in the Roman Empire.[52] From now on, Foucault notices, the emphasis is on the frailty of the individual facing the ills of sexual activity. Such frailty is conceived in relationship with a more abstract and universal notion of nature and reason. The citizen is called to develop exercises that strengthen his ability to control himself with the goal of enjoyment. Such is

> an art of existence that revolves around the question of the self, of its dependence and independence, of its universal form and of the connection it can and should establish with others, of the procedures by which it exerts its control over itself.[53]

The tradition of the *epimeleia heautou* had been prominent in classical Greece. The new emphasis on this type of care made it an end in itself, not a means to enter the political structure. Whereas in previous times ruling one's self was a pre-condition to being able to rule the other, in late antiquity the control of oneself, following the Stoic tradition, became an end in itself. Additionally, there came to be an increased anxiety about the dangers of sex because the self, now conceived as a weak entity, is in need of continuous therapy that is provided partly by philosophical practice that, in turn, helps in the task of providing an ordered pattern to one's actions in concordance with the world order around us.

As in classical Athens, subjectification is characterized as a free choice made by free individuals to give oneself a certain form: a specific aesthetic. That is, ethics is concerned with modeling oneself to achieve the optimal self, not with abiding by a set of universal rules. The ethical subject works on himself to achieve a more beautiful selfhood. It is this aspect that, in Foucault's view, separates these modes of ethics from what Christianity would bring to the table with its pastoral surveillance of the ethical content:

> one will then attempt to regulate everything – positions, frequency, gestures, each partner's state of mind, knowledge by the one of the intentions of the other, signs of desire on one side, tokens of acceptance of the other, and so on. For its part, Hellenistic and Roman moral philosophy says little on this subject.[54]

Foucault argues that five centuries after Plato, whose thought in the *Alcibiades* Foucault analyzed in volume two of the *History of Sexuality*, Seneca, Plutarch, Epictetus, and other Stoics addressed the same problems, although the solutions have a totally different significance: the *care sui* in the Imperial period, unlike in Classical Greek, is a universal principle that does not demand a political self. In effect, whereas in Greek thought ruling oneself and ruling others were inextricably intertwined, the above-named thinkers consider that taking care of the self demands an abandonment of the political realm. Furthermore, what in Plato had a pedagogical undertone here becomes medical care in the sense that one has to become the doctor of oneself. One of the technologies implemented to achieve these goals is the cultivation of pedagogical silence and a proper education in the art of listening.

Foucault seems to have his eyes set on later Christian practices when he specifies Seneca's understanding of self-examination as a technique geared towards the purification of conscience, closely following the Pythagorean tradition. What is particular to the Roman approach is that the self is not examined as it would be in a courtroom, but following administrative-like procedures. What later in Christianity would be a review of one's "bad intentions" is here an examination of what one still has left to do, a reminder of the uncompleted task of working on oneself. In *On Anger 3.36*, Seneca recommends the following routine: to reflect on one's day in terms of actions and attitudes and getting a clear idea of the things that could be done better, not with the intention of chastising oneself but with the purpose of administering a better self for tomorrow. In sum, one examines oneself not as a judge scrutinizing what is at fault, but rather as an administrator concerned with acquiring better skills to complete the task at hand.

Christianity substituted the "care of the self" for "knowing oneself," thus shifting the focus from self-cultivation geared towards obtaining freedom to self-discovery as a means to salvation in the next life. Foucault explores the techniques that the Stoics implemented to show how *care sui* was based on a series of technologies of the self that were focused on building one's own capacities for reflection rather than on a superior outsider tracking and setting limits to them. Some critics have observed how Foucault's "resurrection" of self-cultivation has the merit of divesting Greek and Roman ethics of the stigma that centuries of Christianity had imposed on them.[55] Foucault later hints at what is the ethical import for the present of his examination of antiquity:

> We find it difficult to base rigorous morality and austere principles on the precept that we should give ourselves more care than anything else in the world. We are more inclined to see taking care of ourselves as an immorality, as a means of escape from all possible rules. We inherit the tradition of Christian morality which makes self-renunciation the condition for salvation. To know oneself was, paradoxically, a means of self-renunciation.[56]

Foucault is interested in exposing a *care sui* capable of counteracting the disciplinary practices that contemporary regimes impose on the self and, at the same time, divesting contemporary notions of subjectivity that conceive of the self as a nuclear entity with a telos. For him,

> the risk of dominating others and exercising a tyrannical power over them arises precisely only when one has not taken care of the self but

has become slave of one's desire. But if you take proper care of yourself (. . .) you cannot abuse your power over others.[57]

Such nod to Christian ethics, however, refers to late antiquity, not to the Christian sources coetaneous with his Roman analysis,[58] like the Book of Revelation, a particularly interesting source because it provides valuable information on the construction of the Self in Early Christianity; it also has the added value that its audience belongs to the "underside" of Empire. The Apocalypse of John represents, in my view, an example of an early construction of selfhood that has the potential to resist (not always in positive ways) contemporary regimes of the normal, while providing a contrapuntal reading of the selfhood that Foucault ascribed to Greco-Roman culture but at the expense of obviating its imperializing political, ethical, and religious structures.[59]

Foucault and early Christianity

That Foucault's influence on the study of the New Testament sources is not voluminous comes as no surprise, given that biblical studies has been reluctant to incorporate post-modernist thought, especially methodologies, into its analysis, but also because Foucault left unfinished (and unpublished) his work on Early Christianity. Yet numerous biblical interpreters have appropriated Foucault's genealogical approach to the study of the New Testament or have tried to extrapolate for specific Christian texts scattered insights dispersed through the three volumes of Foucault's *History of Sexuality*. Paul's epistolary work has drawn the most attention, with authors focusing on his definition of power, his understanding of sexual ethics, and his construction of the self.

Halvor Moxnes has developed a similar project to the one I am proposing in this chapter: "a Foucauldian reading of Paul, but against the position of Foucault on Christian ethics as a set of rules."[60] Moxnes underscores the values of a Foucauldian approach to Pauline literature, such as the ability to scrutinize the formations of the self in Christian writings.[61] Yet Moxnes also identifies some dangers of such an approach: elitism, male chauvinism, and a disregard for the role of the divine in the formation of the self.

Moxnes accurately summarizes Foucault's theorization of the difference between pagan and Christian ethics and throws into relief the highly influential idea that the gap was not about sexual norms but about the self and its relationship with itself as a "desiring man." Moxnes condenses Foucault's views by noticing that, for the Greeks, life was a mixture of pleasure and desire, while for the Christians desire was to be avoided. Furthermore, in pagan ethics, moral obligation took the form of political and aesthetic choices, whereas for Christians it was divine law. The Greeks used different techniques (techne) to rule their body and their household as a way to shape their morality; the Christians resort to scrutiny and confessional practices.

Lastly, the goal of morality for the Greeks was mastery, for the Christians it was purity and immortality.[62] Moxnes attempts a reading of 1 Cor 6:12–20 that addresses each of these four areas of ethics.

Moxnes further faults Foucault (describing it as his "most serious flaw") for not considering that God is not an external authority but that, for Christians, the divinity is part of the core of the self. Moxnes is also extremely useful because he addresses the charges of male chauvinism and elitism thrown at Foucault. However, as I will argue later on, Moxnes stops short of construing the relationship between the formation of the self and Paul as a colonized subject. Moreover, Moxnes rightly criticizes Foucault for applying a later ethos to Paul's work: Foucault certainly overlooked that first-century Christianity was not really concerned with setting a system of rules. However, Moxnes does not properly address what to me is the very accurate Foucauldian insight that Christianity shifted towards an ethos concerned with purity.

Moxnes situates his analyses of 1 Corinthians, and Foucault for that matter, within broader debates on *askesis* and identity. Adopting Valantasis's definition of asceticism as a performance "within a dominant social environment intended to inaugurate a new subjectivity, different social relations, and an alternative symbolic universe," Moxnes points to the conservative nature of the asceticism promoted by the elitist philosophers and thinkers that Foucault features in his three volumes, suggesting ways in which *askesis* might contribute to keep "things in place." In good Foucauldian fashion, he is concerned with an approach to the past that destabilizes the present, more specifically contemporary notions of family/marriage supposedly grounded in biblical morals. Moxnes sees 1 Corinthians as undercutting pagan morals in the sense that he argues that lying with a prostitute creates a unity of the two, thus endangering a male's belonging to the body of Christ.

Regarding the ethical subject, Moxnes suggests that the body is the main area of concern. Paul conceives of the body in relational terms, not as something under the control of the manly self, but as a slave to God, and in this he signals a distinction between the Christian male in general and his peers in Corinth. The "ontological" relationality of the body seems to put it at risk of deviating from proper inclusion into the body of Christ. As Moxnes puts it, "the right askesis, that is, exercise in oneself as an ethical subject, was renunciation of sexual relations in a manner that set the Christian male apart from commonly accepted norms of masculinity in the Graeco-Roman society of Corinth."[63] The goal of asceticism is thus to be a part of the Lord's body.

Moxnes concludes by pointing out how Paul's conception of the body inaugurates "a new subjectivity" in that it antagonizes pagan views that do not see certain sexual acts as affecting one's self. Asceticism becomes the path to keep the body as belonging to Christ, because it places the body exclusively in the world of God. Askesis consequently also results in depreciation of the value of marriage.[64] Moxnes seems to suggest that the "heteronomy" introduced by the human-divinity relationship undermines Greco-Roman aspirations to mastery of the self while undoing ontological claims about the body. For Moxnes, the Pauline conception of the body signals that it belongs somewhere else or, better said, to someone else. Furthermore, the body has no "essence," no "ontological identity," because it is embedded in relationships that, essentially, define its nature. And, finally and more importantly, the "primary determination of the male body is that it is a member of Christ's body.[65]

Moxnes's reading of Paul through Foucault but against Foucault himself offers remarkable insights both in terms of methodology and exegesis. In terms of method, Moxnes makes use of Foucault's genealogical approach in order to throw into relief a conception of the self that has the potential to inform strategies of resistance in the present. On the one hand, Paul's understanding of the body as a relational entity may be interpreted as an antidote against Roman elitism and hypermasculinity, while having the potential to undo the "dandyism" that many critics see in Foucault's explanation of the past. That is, Paul's relational ontology (at least, in Moxnes's version) poses a challenge to a Roman aesthetics of the self that can evolve into dilettantism (at least, in Foucault's rendering).[66] On the other hand, the consequences of such an understanding pose a challenge to contemporary understandings of the biblical past as a religion invested in marriage and family. Exegetically speaking, Moxnes's approach advances an understanding of a "Pauline self" that accounts for the relation between identity and sexual acts: a certain "sexual practice," Paul argues, reconfigures the self.

In what follows, I approach Revelation taking some of these methodological and exegetical steps. Although Revelation belongs to a different strand of Christianity than Pauline literature, there are numerous elements that lend themselves to a Foucauldian approach. However, there are at least two elements that I add to Moxnes's approach. First, I take full consideration of the "colonized self." Revelation (and Paul, I would argue) provides us with a unique opportunity to theorize the "self" as a counterbalance to Foucault's elite. Second, although I agree with Moxnes that Foucault's understanding of Christianity as a set of rules is totally misplaced, I also think that Moxnes underplays one important insight: Christianity brought the concern for purity to the forefront.

Revelation: a Foucauldian approach

Scholars typically study the construction of gender and sexuality in Revelation by analyzing gender imagery (literary studies), by studying comparative gender ideologies (historic-critical exegesis and socio-scientific approaches), or by attending to discursive gender formation (ideological analysis).[67] I build on this scholarship to propose a different, but complementary, approach: a Foucauldian approach to subject formation. My goal is to survey technologies of selfhood in the Apocalypse with two objectives in mind: first, to explore ways in which resistance, broadly conceived, can be re-appropriated in the present; and, second, to initiate a reflection on the links between subject formation, resistance, and sexual symbolism that, in turn, shall introduce the topic of the Great Whore of Babylon in chapter 3.

This chapter started by addressing the question of bodily resistance in the context of the present Empire and then transitioned to an exploration of embodied subjectivity in antiquity as theorized by Foucault. Such an approach proves extremely useful to think about the ethics of the Apocalypse because it engages a "historiographical style" that bridges the gap, so prominent in Biblical Studies, between the past and the present, history and ethics, exegesis and hermeneutics. The question pursued, then, is whether "revelatory ethics," conceived as the exploration of how the self relates to itself, can offer a deconstructive/destabilizing project for the present. In the second section, I introduced Halvor Moxnes's study of Paul's conception on the body in order to show the usefulness of applying such an approach to the New Testament textual corpus. In what follows, I pursue an analogous study of ethics in the book of Revelation, but with two important additional concerns. First, I take seriously the assumption that the self in Revelation is a colonized self. I argue that the "colonized self" offers an important counterbalance to the elitism of Foucault's sources. Second, I explore Foucault's insight that Christianity introduced a concern for purity that resulted in a crucial shift in ethics in Western thought. This shift is crucial to understanding the metaphor of the Whore in Chapters 17–18. I focus on Rev 14:1–5 to address these questions.

The colonized self in Revelation

More than any other book in the New Testament, Revelation's theology, ideology, and composition are determined by the relationship Empire-Community. Revelation, whether one thinks of it as resistant or imperial literature, is shaped from beginning to end by its positioning towards the Roman Empire. Scholarship has addressed many aspects of this relationship, such as historical, literary, and discursive links between Roman imperializing politics and the emergence of the new religious movement. Most of these studies, however, are concerned with a study of the ethics of Revelation as conceived within the Enlightenment paradigm. That is, they explore the possibility of extracting rules, strategies of action, for the present while evaluating its ethical import. Here I approach "revelatory ethics" as a project that explores how the process of colonization oversaturated selfhood formation, how the relationship of the self to itself – following Foucault's insights – is mediated by the political reality of Empire.

The self in Revelation is deeply split between two worlds: the world of Empire and the utopian kingdom. The result of this split is, I contend, a deeply confrontational, oppositional, and agonistic selfhood. Selfhood is caught up between the impossibility of forging what is desirable, the fall of Rome, and the emerging of the new City. The conflict between these two political realities (with their respective actions, characters, places, values) takes place at a cosmic level, staging a drama of epic proportions that determines, and is determined by, how selfhood is conceived. Adela Yarbro Collins has even suggested that this drama shapes a schizophrenic self that needs to be accounted for, explained, and progressively disavowed.[68]

Many of the selfhood features that Moxnes traced in the Pauline literature are prevalent in Revelation.[69] The interpreter of Revelation soon realizes that Foucault's understanding of Early Christianity as an ethical system fixed on rules does not apply to Revelation, as it does not apply to Pauline literature. There are hardly any moral prescriptions to be found in the Apocalypse, and most ethical and moral aspects are conveyed more in descriptive than normative fashion. John seems to be more concerned with criticizing or sanctioning specific practices within the communities he is addressing than with setting up universal moral rules. For instance, his address to the seven churches in Asia Minor concerns itself with reinforcing or condemning actions depending on how they promote certain group identity. It seems, as I will show, that a specific notion of purity drives John in his exhortations to the communities.

Revelation does not promote in any shape or form a compliance with household mores as imagined in Roman imperial ideology. Moxnes's observation than Paul's asceticism contravenes the kind of "conservative asceticism" that can be found in Roman sources also applies to Revelation. The self is not designed to peacefully fit in a larger social or political schema. Rev 14:4, for instance, poses an agonistic self, set not only against the imperial self but also against the adversary cosmic enemy. Several features are attributed to the 144,000: they have tattooed on their foreheads the name of the Lamb and his Father; they are the only ones able to learn the song in order to worship in the heavenly court; they have not defiled themselves with women "for they are virgins" (Rev 14:4); they follow the Lamb wherever he goes; and finally, they have been purchased among the men as first fruits. Such agonistic dimension is evinced by the positioning of the chosen as the anti-image of the devotees of the beast (Empire).[70] Moreover, the chosen also stand in opposition to those who figure negatively in the cosmic drama. Drawing literary connections between Revelation and Enoch, Olson concludes that "the redeemed 144,000 stand in radical opposition to the fallen angels of the BW."[71] It seems, Olson argues further, that the priestly imagery deployed in 14:1–5, such as their exclusive musical function, is designed to antagonize the deficient priests, those fallen angels that betrayed their role by getting involved with earthly women.[72]

Despite being completely unexplored in Revelation Studies (but also, as I have shown, in Pauline Studies), selfhood cannot be fully understood outside of the process of colonization. The colonized psyche is a requirement of any colonization process and, as Fanon has taught us, the measurement to its success. He argues that

> in the colonial world, the colonized's affectivity is kept on edge like a running sore flinching from a caustic agent. And the psyche retracts, is obliterated, and finds an outlet through muscular spasms that have caused many an expert to classify the colonized as hysterical.[73]

It is particularly interesting here that Fanon blurs the distinction between the political, the somatic, and the psychological. The violence exerted by the colonizer not only affects the division between the infrastructure and the super-structure but also shatters that same distinction by conceiving of the colonized body as a battlefield where even breathing is occupied. Fanon poignantly argues that it is not the soil that is the object of occupation, but the subjects themselves. As he elaborates,

> there is not occupation of territory, on the one hand, and independence of persons on the other. It is the country as a whole, its history, its daily pulsation that are contested, disfigured, in the hope of a final destruction. Under these conditions, the individual's breathing is an observed, and occupied breathing. It is a combat breathing.[74]

Revelation thinks about the colonized self through the deprived self that dreams of a utopian future. Revelation portrays a cosmic drama that believers are encouraged to bear in order to remain faithful to the Lamb and worthy of entering the Heavenly Jerusalem. In Rev 7:1–17, when the four angels are about to destroy the earth, there is a call for the chosen to be sealed so they are not killed. Immediately afterwards, a great universal multitude whose role is to worship appears before the throne "in white robes" and holding "palm branches." They are the ones who have experienced great tribulation, and consequently they are promised that they will not experience hunger, thirst, heat, or any kind of hardship. In the midst of a cosmic war, their leader takes the "multitude" to the "springs of water" where "God will wipe every tear from their eyes." (7:17).

Deprivation is balanced out by God's beneficial actions to the believer whose identity is, in the end, shaped by his (the self is, after all, male) reliance on the divinity's plans. The source of identity is, as Moxnes puts it, heteronomously conferred. Here the relationship of the self to itself dramatically departs from the models that Foucault mapped in the Greco-Roman sources. For one, the colonized self draws on a tradition that confers dignity through the role of priesthood and kingship (1:6; 5:10; 20:6). At the same time, the strong identity achieved through being a member of a chosen group brings about an extremely strong set of disavowals – Rev 17–18 suggests an indictment on trading practices, alcohol, sex, luxury, etc. – that have important consequences for understanding the role of Babylon, the Great Whore, as a trope for identity formation.

Whereas it is true, as Stephen Moore and Chris Frilingos have convincingly argued, that every aspect of the Apocalypse's symbolism is shaped after imperial ideology,[75] it is also the case that John is fashioning a new subjectivity in light of cruel deprivation. The muscular God, to say it with Moore,[76] is the symptom of a colonized mind, but it is not necessarily the final solution offered by the deprived psyche. Does imperial power trickle down to the inner, most intimate aspects of the process of subject formation in Revelation? What does the colonized self see reflected when it looks into the imperial mirror? John does not seem to see imperial power as emanating from a hub, as stemming from a centrally located root, as irradiating its influence from monadic core, but rather as distributed among diverse parties. The Whore, in this reading, stands not simply for the center of Empire (Rome), its holder (Emperor), but is a metaphor that translates the capillary nature of empire itself: "she has become a dwelling place for demons," "a haunt for every unclean spirit," "a haunt for every unclean and detestable beast," (18:1). Furthermore, John implies in his addresses that all nations complicit in the deleterious effects of its power have partaken of that power when he encourages them to "come out of her" (18:4).

On the topic of the thematization of power, "revelatory ethics" resembles Hardt and Negri's Foucauldian theorization of imperial power as governance, rooted in a series of supranational assemblages, as a political modality of power that is disseminated beyond the nation-state and its bureaucratic apparatuses through networks of control that are disseminated both globally and contextually.[77] Theoretical identifications of governance with neoliberalism notwithstanding, John's depiction of the Great Whore sitting "on peoples, multitudes, nations, and languages" (17:15) signals the diffuse and totalizing dimension of imperial power itself with "the multitude" – quite literally in this verse – as the other side of it. John's conceptualization of the self and its political clout is, however, nothing like the Multitude. For Hardt and Negri, the subject, the "agent of biopolitical production and resistance" is called to a "militancy of love" Francis of Assisi-style where "the communist militant" advances a joyous life because there is no outside, only an inside that "is the productive cooperation of mass intellectually and affective networks."[78] Revelation, to the contrary, defines the subject, despite the capillary nature of Empire, from "his" call to come out of Empire (18:4) and look at its demise from the outside (18:20). Revelation's multitude, defined in masculinist terms as it is, represents a "theological exodus" – not the ambiguous anthropological migration described by Hardt and Negri – at odds and in deep conflict with the political community it seeks departure from. Unlike the "concrete invention of a first new place in the non-place," the multitude is the envisioning of a new place (heaven and earth) in a divine place, the imaginative exercise of emancipation of a colonized mind that is still in the non-place of Empire.

The self and the whore

The destiny of the Great Whore of Babylon in Rev 17–18 is not unlike the destinies of other women in the book of Revelation. Revelation is a text filled with violence against the gendered and sexual other. The strategy of annihilating the sexual other (see Jezebel) helps to delineate the limits of the community, while shaping a selfhood deeply rooted in the value of purity. John's concern for purity is evident in numerous descriptions – the Holy City (Rev 21:27), the garments of the saints (7:4; 15:6; 19:8; 22:14), and the Great Whore as the haunt of unclean spirits (18:2). In this regard, Revelation shares many features with Paul's representation of the body. John bans any connection with Jezebel, as he will with Babylon, because the cosmic war is also a war against fornication. Scholars agree that Revelation's stance toward Jezebel signals a broader uncompromising stance towards imperial mores.[79] Very much like Paul, therefore, John sees in the defiled body of the woman a threat to a political project that sets purity at the center of the agenda.[80]

Jacob Neusner has shown how in Judaism purity was gradually detached from Temple cult and acquired ethical undertones becoming almost synonymous with virtue. Impurity referred to everything that God rejected, mostly pagan worship, sexual acts, or nutrition mores.[81] All of these aspects are clearly visible in Revelation, where John's project of boundary-definition seeks an uncompromising stance towards Empire. Revelation's concern with purity shows especially in 14:1–5, where John views the Lamb staying on Mount Zion with his army of 144,000 males who have not defiled themselves with women. In 14:8 an angel announces Babylon the Great, portrayed as a feminine entity that has intoxicated the nations with her "porneia." Postcolonial theory argues that women bear the burden of being the gatekeepers of purity in the relationship between colonizing and colonized powers. Rev 14:5 places the burden of keeping purity on the male community. In Revelation's symbolic world, women can be only virgins or whores.

The epic/martial rhetoric leads many interpreters to see the 144,000 as participating in Holy War. The immediate textual reference is Dt 23:9–10, where warfare demands sexual abstinence. However, as Olson rightly notices, sexual abstinence is not the same as virginity.[82] In the previous section, I mentioned how the virgins "are an anti-image not only to the devotees of the beast, but also, it seems, to the fallen angels."[83] In this reading, "the chosen" function as a replacement of the angels that abandoned their place and got involved with women. Since the watchers forsook their virginity, stepping out of their proper sphere, John is proposing an army of pure priests, a renewed heavenly priesthood. Olson prudently notices that a literary reference to BW grants little information about John's intended audience. What is important, however, is that John deploys the literary reference because it serves well his broader concern of purity and advances the idea of discipleship as something "apart" from Empire. John seems to agree with the widespread idea that the "redeemed" will become angels.[84]

The portrayal of the Great Whore shares numerous elements with Jezebel: they are both whores; their offspring is demonic; they are voracious; and they consume defiling food.[85] These similarities notwithstanding, the image of Babylon is arguably more complex. Revelation 17 situates John as witness in a court trial. Chapter 17:1 has the angel inviting John to witness the "judgment of the great harlot." Although the trial focuses on Babylon, many other characters are subjected to trial. The allies of the Great Whore, those who have sinned with her, could be interpreted as those whom Foucault analyzed in volumes 2 and 3 of *History of Sexuality*. From this perspective, one can see how a slippage is happening where the focus is not so much on the relationship of the self to itself as to the actual facts. Thus, fornication comes to define an effeminizing trait that goes beyond its explicit sexual meaning and refers to any action/value/attitude that threatens the identity of the believer as John has conceived of it: table customs, trade rituals, sexual practices, and political alliances.

In Paul, the ethical substance is the male body, conceived as a permeable multivalent reality open to transformation. If in 14:4 Revelation insisted on the need not to be defiled with women, one could possibly argue that the pollution here has become specific in the shape of a "whore." It is worth noticing, however, that, unlike in the Graeco-Roman world portrayed by Foucault, there is little emphasis on the body understood as an individual, personal, monadic entity. In Revelation, the cosmic war, Manichean as it is, brings focus to communal bodies rather than to personal bodies. Dale Martin, for instance, has carefully analyzed how in Pauline Christianity the problem with *porneia* is of communal significance.[86] As Moxnes puts it when analyzing 1 Cor,

> the prostitute becomes a symbol of 'fornication,' which takes on cosmological dimensions as the opposite of 'the Lord.' Therefore, sexual relations with a prostitute are removed from the area of male morality in the Graeco-Roman context and become a question of placing oneself in the cosmic battle between God and his opponents (. . .) In Paul's discourse such relations become the ultimate danger for a Christian man; they represented not superiority, but resulted in a fateful unity with a prostitute and with the world of opposition to God. The only way to preserve masculinity, 'his own body' was therefore to "shun fornication.'[87]

In Revelation 17–18, the ethical substance takes the constitution of the communal body for granted and seeks to reinforce its identity by disavowing any link between the community and the heads of the political empire as well as its inhabitants. The disidentification with Empire via sexual imagery prepares the audience for the final defeat of earthly powers in Rev 19:17–21.

The Great Whore is a central figure not only because of her actions but also because of the actions others have with her. Previous observations on *porneia* and the harlot in Paul fully apply to Rev 17–18: the figure of the Whore displaces sexual relations from the realm of the personal onto the cosmic. The Whore comes to represent everything that opposes the Lamb (17:14): drunkenness, fornication, excess, blasphemy, and impurity. Furthermore, Babylon comes to represent everything that the self needs to disavow.

John, however, goes beyond Paul in his stigmatization of the whore and exacerbates the consequences that mixing with the whore have for the community. John, like Paul, is concerned with the desiring body but in a much more negative way. Revelation focuses on the disastrous consequences of having any contact with the Whore and any of her acolytes. Revelation displaces any kind of sexual desire and converts it into a political desire to topple the Whore. One could possibly say that "toppling a whore" is no longer conceptualized as sexual desire but as a political aspiration. In Rev 18:3 John shows how all the nations are contaminated by their fornication with the Whore. The kings and the merchants are chastised for having had interactions with her. The exhortation is clear: "Come out from her, my people, that you may not participate in her sins and you may not receive of her plagues" (Rev 18:4).

The Whore is portrayed as an entity of unlimited desire and thus as the anti-type of the self whose desire is geared towards the heavenly reality. The desire to give one's life a beautiful form is here abandoned in order to participate in the life of the heavenly community through following of the Lamb. John crafts the image of the whore in order to shape his readers' ideological, religious, political, and economical commitments. On the negative side, disidentification needs to happen at every level of selfhood formation; on the positive side, the self is to be reshaped by following the Lamb and participating in his victory.

The ethical work continues to be ascetical. Whereas Paul exhorts his reader to "flee from fornication" (1 Cor 6:18), John insists that "my people" come out of her (18:4). Askesis, however, once more becomes radicalized in Revelation for, unlike Paul, John suggests a complete abandonment of any imperial way of life. Although John does not directly address his readers, he deploys a series of images and metaphors that aim to shape his readers' attitudes and morals. Consider, for instance, how the angel portrays the demise of Babylon as the end of a luxurious lifestyle: no more music, craftsmanship, labor, or marriage.[88] As numerous critics point out, one of the reasons John condemns the whore is because she represents the worship of wealth and luxury.[89]

The ethical dimension of telos is found in the call to disidentify with the Whore as a trope of imperial reality, in the command to transcending the earthly realm and attaining a new divine reality. Right after the defeat of the Great Whore, Revelation narrates the rejoicing in heaven because those "who make it" are to marry the Lamb. If in Paul the body is not for fornication, and if such abstinence results in a union with the body of Christ, then in Revelation the body becomes part of the bride that marries the Lamb (Rev 19:8–9).

There are two aspects that are worth expanding upon after the demise of the Great Whore: the multitude occupies the center stage and it is, to some extent, feminized. There is hardly any room for individuality in Revelation. Once the imperial reality has been banished the multitude rejoices in heaven (19:1.6) and becomes the Bride. The self in Revelation ends up being both communal and feminine but only because it has been purified of any imperial contamination.[90] The saints become the woman that marries the Lamb. Consequently, the bride is a collective entity (since it is also a city) formed by those who have been able to stay clear of imperial contamination. The wedding results in the coming of the kingdom of God. The vision of the bride in Chapter 21 starts with a utopian proclamation: "a new heaven and a new earth appear for the first heaven and the first earth have gone away." (21:1). The appearance of the bride is related to the elimination of the things that include death, sorrow, and pain (v.4) and that are now possible because of the demise of Rome, and because there has been a call to keep the self from its contamination.[91]

Conclusion

Tom Nairn considers that Hardt and Negri's theorization of the multitude

> summons the great, multitudinous nation of mankind to join in an even greater encounter with the Absolute, a last Day of living Judgment where all will be redeemed. Globalization is merely the wave bearing everyone towards this end. It's the vindication of old mystical intuitions of oneness and reconciliation with heaven, brought to fruition unexpectedly by capitalism's post-1989 world reach.[92]

Such a call to be a part of the contemporary multitude shares some features with Revelation's invitation to overturn Empire. I have shown how Revelation conceives of selfhood as a communal entity antagonistically posed against the reality of the Roman Empire, displacing the desire to belong to this world onto a utopian future "outside" Imperium. Revelation theorizes Empire as an extensive and intensive reality that seeks to configure the process of subject formation and, consequently, offers a global alternative to Rome's inhuman demands.

The effects of Rome on subject formation as conceptualized by Revelation resemble the way Empire shapes contemporary identities. In Hardt and Negri's view, Empire's biopower produces a subjectivity that serves capitalism's interests, while creating the possibility for the Multitude to use power networks to envision and create a world that pushes Empire beyond its limits. Revelation poses an emergent resistant subjectivity to Empire that counters a monadic conception of selfhood, while imagining a utopian alternative that is not outside of political empire but built from within. John not only provides a global strategy to resist imperialism, but also shapes a communal subjectivity that seeks to carve out an imagined space oriented towards a new utopia.

Accordingly, Revelation can be interpreted as an example of under-history, to agree with Foucault, that undoes historical unity; a counter-example, a genealogy of selfhood that counters the imperial self. This notion of selfhood comes, however, with some risks that call for further deconstruction. It is not the case that the Apocalypse creates a confessional self, but it is true that purity becomes a concern that plays a central role in the configuration of desire. As I show in the next chapter, subject formation in Revelation calls for a questioning of sexual stereotyping, especially as it relates to nation building.

Notes

1 Michael Hardt and Antonio Negri, *Empire* (Cambridge, MA: Harvard University Press, 2000).
2 Michael Hardt, *Multitude: War and Democracy in the Age of Empire* (New York: Penguin Press), 2004; Antonio Negri, *Reflections on Empire* (Cambridge, MA; Malden, UK: Polity, 2008), Michael Hardt, and Antonio Negri, *Commonwealth* (Cambridge: Belknap Press of Harvard University Press, 2009).
3 I understand that Marxist-inspired liberationist projects both in philosophy and in theology and more specifically in Biblical Studies have made a groundbreaking contribution; they are, however, notably outdated. This is especially true in the field of Biblical Studies, where, after the decline of the metanarratives and historical successes of the Left, Postcolonial Studies and other postmodern approaches to Scripture have failed to provide a clear connection between readers and Scripture and, more importantly, have failed to provide a new framework from which to read Scripture now that the previous model of Empire has declined, if not disappeared.
4 The rich contributions debating the core theoretical notions and the implications of their subsequent practical applications developed by Hardt and Negri in *Empire*, *Multitude*, and *Commonwealth* go beyond the narrow scope of the present chapter. For a general overview of these engagements, see: Pierre Lamarche, David Sherman, and Max Rosenkrantz, *Reading Negri: Marxism in the Age of Empire*, Volume 3 of Creative Marxism (Chicago: Open Court, 2011); Bruce Ellis Benson, and Peter Goodwin Heltzel, eds., *Evangelicals and Empire: Christian Alternatives to the Political Status Quo* (Grand Rapids, MI: Brazos Press, 2008); Timothy S. Murphy, and Abdul-Karim Mustapha, *Resistance in Practice: The Philosophy of Antonio Negri* (London: Pluto Press, 2005); Bogdana Koljevic, *Twenty-First Century Biopolitics* (Austria: Peter Lang GmbH, 2015).
5 One could reasonably argue that the reasons to feature Empire as the starting and prominent point – its comprehensive theorization of the global, the conceptualization of bodily resistance and its relationship to justice, and the heuristic contribution to bridge the historiographical gap – could equally demand the incorporation of different, whether parallel, supplementary, or oppositional, theoretical trajectories. For instance, Atilio Boron's detailed contestation of the assumptions, developments, and conclusions of Hardt and Negri's intervention

offsets, from the perspective of the Global South, a predominantly Western view of globalization; Atilio Borón, *Empire and Imperialism: A Critical Reading of Michael Hardt and Antonio Negri* (London; New York: Zed Books, 2005). However, the ultimate goal of situating the emancipatory potential of Revelation within the challenges that contemporary globalization poses to subject formation and subjectivity does not demand a full-blown philosophical ascription to a specific theory of empire. Although indebted to their contributions, especially in its Foucauldian theorization of power, my presentation of Empire frames the topic at hand but does not reflect a justification of Hardt and Negri's insights. In other words, a different trajectory of analysis might yield similar results for the purposes of the present investigation. For instance, Wendy Brown's sustained critique of contemporary neoliberal governance – its undoing of democratic citizenship, its proposal of instrumental reason, its privatization of every sphere of the public sphere, etc. – calls for a restoration of the *homo politicus* while simultaneously being aware of the lack of substantial alternatives left by the rationality of the *homo economicus*. My project, as it shall become clearer in the following chapters, draws on the cultural, religious, political, and anthropological influence of the biblical texts to craft "local knowledges and achieve the local control essential to human thriving and ecological stewardship in the context of any worldwide economic system" without ascribing to a thick description and theorization of what how? the "neo-empire" works; Wendy Brown, *Undoing the Demos: Neoliberalism's Stealth Revolution* (New York; Cambridge: Zone Books, 2015), 220–21. See also R.A.W. Rhodes, *Understanding Governance: Policy Networks, Governance, Reflexivity, and Accountability*, Public Policy and Management (Buckingham; Philadephia: Open University Press, 1997). Pierre Dardot, and Christian Laval, *The New Way of the World: On Neoliberal Society* (London; New York: Verso, 2013).

6　Hardt and Negri, *Commonwealth*, xii–xiii.
7　David B. Abernethy, *The Dynamics of Global Dominance: European Overseas Empires, 1415–1980* (New Haven, CT: Yale University Press, 2000), 20.
8　Philip Pomper, "The History and Theory of Empires," *History and Theory* 44, no. 4 (2005): 2.
9　"Empire is "configured ab initio as a dynamic and flexible systemic structure." Hardt and Negri, *Commonwealth*, 13.
10　Hardt and Negri, *Commonwealth*, 232.
11　Ibid., 233.
12　Negri, *Reflections on Empire*, 308.
13　"Against the modern European conceptions of sovereignty, which consigned political power to a transcendent realm and thus estranged and alienated the sources of power from society, here the concept of sovereignty refers to a power entirely within society. Politics is not opposed to but integrates and completes society," Ibid., 164.
14　Ibid., 315.
15　Ibid., 182.
16　Hardt and Negri, *Commonwealth*, 59.
17　*Empire*, 198.
18　"Disciplinary society is that society in which social command is constructed through a diffuse network of *dispositifs* or apparatuses that produce and regulate customs, habits, and productive practices (. . .) in which mechanisms of command become ever more 'democratic,' ever more immanent to the social field, distributed throughout the brains and bodies of the citizens" (Ibid., 23).
19　Ibid.
20　In the society of control biopower is the exclusive terrain of reference (Ibid., 24).

21 Ibid.
22 Ibid., 41.
23 Ibid., 196–97.
24 Ibid., 198.
25 Ibid., 320–24.
26 Ibid., 216–18.
27 Michel Foucault, "The Subject of Power," *Critical Inquiry* 8, no. 4 (1982): 777–95.
28 For instance, Gramsci notably theorized that hegemony works by making people believe "against their own interests." For Foucault, the problem with this approach is that it presupposes a right vision (that can be taught to those who have bought into a false consciousness) and it denies any agency to the subject itself.
29 He coins the expression "descending individualism" to explain how in discipli-nary societies, unlike in feudal times, people are more individuated the lower in the social ladder they are.
30 Michel Foucault, *The History of Sexuality. Vol. 1: An Introduction* (New York: Vantage, 1990), 95–7.
31 Michel Foucault, Mauro Bertani, Alessandro Fontana, François Ewald, and David Macey, *Society Must Be Defended: Lectures at the Collège De France, 1975–76*, 1st ed. (New York: Picador, 2003), 7.
32 Ibid.
33 Ibid., 179.
34 Ibid., 69–70.
35 Ibid., 66.
36 Ibid., 68.
37 Ibid., 66. For Foucault, the role of history remains untouched until the rise of the race-war history. This Roman way of doing history, Foucault suggests, finds its counter-discourse in the Bible; ibid., 71.
38 José Medina, "Toward a Foucaultian Epistemology of Resistance: Counter-Memory, Epistemic Friction, and Guerrilla Pluralism," *Foucault Studies* no. 12 (2011): 9–35.
39 Foucault, "The Subject of Power," 785.
40 Michel Foucault, *The History of Sexuality. Vol. 2: The Use of Pleasure* (New York Vintage Books, 1990), 42.
41 Ibid., 26.
42 "On the Genealogy of Ethics," in *Ethics: Subjectivity and Truth*, ed. Paul Rabi-now (New York: New Press, 1997), 263.
43 Ibid., 265.
44 Ibid.
45 Foucault, *The History of Sexuality. Vol. 2*, 54. "The sexual austerity that was prematurely recommended by Greek philosophy is not rooted in the timeless-ness of a law that would take the historically diverse forms of repression, one after the other. It belongs to a history that is more decisive for comprehending the transformations of moral experience than the history of codes: a history of 'ethics,' understood as the elaboration of a form of relation to self that enables an individual to fashion himself into a subject of ethical conduct" (Ibid., 251).
46 "We could say that classical antiquity's moral reflection concerning the pleas-ures was not directed toward a codification of acts, nor toward a hermeneutics of the subject, but toward a stylization of attitudes and aesthetics of existence. A stylization, because the rarefaction of sexual activity presented itself as a sort of open-ended requirement (Ibid., 92).
47 Timothy O'Leary, *Foucault: The Art of Ethics* (London; New York: Continuum, 2002), 65.

48 John J. Winkler, *The Constraints of Desire: The Anthropology of Sex and Gender in Ancient Greece* (New York: Routledge, 1990), 182.
49 Michel Foucault, *The History of Sexuality. Vol. 2*, 70.
50 Michel Foucault, *The History of Sexuality. Vol. 3: The Care of the Self* (New York: Vintage Books, 2002), 66.
51 Ibid., 61.
52 Ibid., 101–17.
53 Ibid., 238.
54 Ibid., 165.
55 "One of the great merits of Foucault's excavation of the Hellenistic practices of the self lies in the way it frees the reception of this tradition from the incrustations of Christian polemics. He demonstrates that Christianity wrongly interprets Hellenistic self-cultivation as closely connected, either historically or analytically, with a 'conceited ontology' that gives license to various brands of hyper-individualism"; Michael Ure, "Senecan Moods: Foucault and Nietzsche on the Art of the Self," *Foucault Studies* 19–52, no. 4 (2007): 23.
56 Michel Foucault, Luther H. Martin, Huck Gutman, and Patrick H. Hutton, *Technologies of the Self: A Seminar with Michel Foucault* (Amherst: University of Massachusetts Press, 1988), 22.
57 Michel Foucault, "The Ethics of the Concern of the Self as a Practice of Freedom," in *Ethics: Subjectivity and Truth*, ed. Paul Rabinow (New York: New Press, 1997), 29.
58 Halvor Moxnes, "Asceticism and Christian Identity in Antiquity: A Dialogue with Foucault and Paul," *Journal for the Study of the New Testament* 26, no. 1 (2003): 8.
59 A critique leveled on completely different terms by Charles Taylor; See Charles Taylor, *Sources of the Self: The Making of the Modern Identity* (Cambridge, MA: Harvard University Press, 1989), 488–90.
60 Moxnes, "Asceticism and Christian Identity in Antiquity," 17.
61 See also Valérie Nicolet-Anderson, *Constructing the Self: Thinking with Paul and Michel Foucault* (Tübingen: Mohr Siebeck, 2012); Elizabeth Anne Castelli, *Imitating Paul: A Discourse of Power* (Louisville: Westminster John Knox Press, 1991).
62 Ibid., 16.
63 Ibid., 22.
64 Moxnes suggests that "The right askesis, that is, exercise in oneself as an ethical subject, was renunciation of sexual relations in a manner that set the Christian male apart from commonly accepted norms of masculinity in the Graeco-Roman society of Corinth" (Ibid.).
65 Ibid., 23.
66 O'Leary, *Foucault*, 93.
67 See bibliography in Chapter 1.
68 Adela Yarbro Collins, *Crisis and Catharsis: The Power of the Apocalypse*, 1st ed. (Philadelphia: Westminster Press, 1984), 154–57.
69 The project of advancing a Foucauldian ethics on New Testament writings goes beyond the scope of the present project. My goal here is rather to signal some common developments in Early Christianity that counterbalance the elitism found in Greco-Roman sources studied by Foucault.
70 The opposition between followers of the Lamb and followers of the Beast stands at many levels: Mount Zion (14:1) stands in contrast to the sea (13:1), the Beast is the anti-image of the Lamb (5:6 vs. 13:3), the worshipers of the Lamb stand in contrast to the worshipers of the Beast (13:8.12). The mark of the lamb stands in contraposition to the mark of the Beast (13:16–17).

71 Daniel C. Olson, " 'Those Who Have Not Defiled Themselves with Women': Revelation 14:4 and the Book of Enoch," *Catholic Biblical Quarterly* 59, no. 3 (1997): 500.
72 Ibid., 501.
73 Fanon, *The Wretched of the Earth*, 19.
74 Ibid., 65.
75 Stephen Moore, *Empire and Apocalypse: Postcolonialism and the New Testament*, Bible in the Modern World v. 12 (Sheffield, UK: Sheffield Phoenix Press, 2006).
76 Stephen Moore, "The Beatific Vision as a Posing Exhibition: Revelation's Hypermasculine Deity," *Journal for the Study of the New Testament* 18, no. 60 (1996): 27–55.
77 See also Brown, *Undoing the Demos*, 115–50.
78 *Empire*, 413.
79 Paul Brooks Duff, *Who Rides the Beast? Prophetic Rivalry and the Rhetoric of Crisis in the Churches of the Apocalypse* (Oxford; New York: Oxford University Press, 2001), 131–32.
80 Mary Douglas has notably theorized the concept of purity in central in social sciences. Her work has informed its theorization in New Testament; Mary Douglas, *Purity and Danger: An Analysis of Concept of Pollution and Taboo*, Routledge Classics (London; New York: Routledge, 2005). See Bruce J. Malina, *The New Testament World: Insights from Cultural Anthropology*, 3rd ed. (Louisville: Westminster John Knox Press, 2001), 170.
81 Jacob Neusner, *The Idea of Purity in Ancient Judaism* (Leiden: Brill, 1973), 13–15.
82 Olson, "Those Who Have Not Defiled Themselves with Women," 495.
83 Ibid., 501.
84 Ibid., 505.
85 Duff, *Who Rides the Beast?* 89–92.
86 Dale B. Martin, *The Corinthian Body* (New Haven: Yale University Press, 1995); Jerome H. Neyrey, *Paul, in Other Words: A Cultural Reading of His Letters*, 1st ed. (Louisville: Westminster; John Knox Press, 1990).
87 Moxnes, "Asceticism and Christian Identity in Antiquity," 22.
88 Craig R. Koester, "Roman Slave Trade and the Critique of Babylon in Revelation 18," *Catholic Biblical Quarterly* 70, no. 4 (2008): 766–86.
89 William Barclay, *The Revelation of John (Vol. 2)* (Louisville: Westminster John Knox Press, 2004), 188.
90 The process of feminization of the self will be expanded in Chapter 4.
91 As Bauckham notices the Bride is clearly contrasted with Babylon; Richard Bauckham, *The Theology of the Book of Revelation* (Cambridge; New York: Cambridge University Press, 1993).
92 Tom Nairn, "Make for the Boondocks," *London Review of Books* 27, no. 9 (2005): 11–14.

3 Thinking sex with the whore of Revelation

Introduction

In the previous chapter, I set the study of Revelation in general, and of the Whore of Babylon in particular, within the contemporary framework of Empire. My goal was twofold: First, at the methodological level, to establish a Foucauldian historiographical model to bridge the gap between the past and the present while keeping the ethical turn at the center of the analysis. Second, at the interpretive level, to approach the Whore of Babylon as a trope of embodied anti-imperial resistance that has emancipatory potential for the present. Understanding Babylon as a building block of anti-imperial subjectivity allowed me to conceive Revelation as a source of resistance for the present.

In this chapter, I explore further the links between the construction of sexuality and resistance to Empire by laying out an analytical framework to explore current correlations between sexual identity and capitalism. Whereas Hardt and Negri's insight that resistance to Empire calls for new ways of envisioning the body triggered Chapter 2's heuristic move, in this chapter I explore the interaction between sexuality and bodily resistance in late capitalism as the heuristic model to look at the ways in which sexual slurs are used to oppose imperial structures in the Hebrew Bible and in Revelation.

First, I set up a contextual theoretical framework to explore the thematic links between bodily resistance and Empire in the present. Second, I use those insights to explore the connection between sexual slurs and imperial resistance in the Hebrew Bible. Third, I compare the connections found with the analysis of Babylon presented in the previous chapter.

Capitalism and sexual identity

Foucault is justly credited with explaining genealogically the cultural coinage of sexual identities and exploring the ways in which contemporary resistance should invent ways of subject formation. However, as many commentators have noticed, Foucault paid little attention to the entanglements of sexual categories with Empire, or to sexuality as a "deployment" of the evolution of late capitalism.

John D'Emilio provides a helpful starting point to think about this relationship between the development of late capitalism and the rise of sexual categorization. D'Emilio begins his analysis by asserting what has become a truism in Queer Theory: That sexual identity (gay and lesbian identity, more precisely) is a product of history, and more explicitly, an outcome of capitalism.[1] D'Emilio connects the unfolding of the labor market in capitalism with the distribution of gender roles and the impact of these phenomena on the creation of sexual identities. He gives a brief history of how capitalism gave birth to the family as a necessary production unit to deliver the next generation of workers – a fundamental process to feed the capitalist machine. While the family was the space of personal life – the realm where personal relationships were nurtured – it remained deeply disconnected from the world of labor and production.[2]

With the incorporation of women into the workforce, along with many other social, political, and scientific developments, including birth control, the household lost its independence as the realm of intimacy, and sexuality became separated from procreation. D'Emilio locates the rise of the gay identity at the point where procreation is uncoupled from the material demands of capitalism for its survival. To put it differently, the dismissal of procreation as the main objective of sex gave rise to other dimensions of sex – one of them being the arrangement of personal affects around it. Sex as reproduction turned into sex as affection. New identities were possible because capitalism freed biology from destiny. This process, however, did not bring about the end of heterosexism and homophobia. D'Emilio notes, while capitalism has debunked the material basis for the nuclear family, it nonetheless conceived of it as the exclusive place of emotional security. At the super-structural level, however, lesbians/gays and other minoritized identities continue to be the scapegoat for the instabilities in the system.[3] Capitalism, D'Emilio concludes, continues to be the problem because it has identified the (heterosexual) family as the privileged site of workforce reproduction.[4] In his view, homophobia and heterosexism will disappear once capitalism is eradicated. Capitalism has fostered a gender division that gave rise to heteronormativity. The gendered division of labor created the gendered division of erotic attachments.

D'Emilio's intuitions have been criticized for being too simplistic, especially in establishing a cause-effect link between the potential abolition of sexuality and the elimination of capitalism. As Hennessy puts it, "capitalism does not require heteronormative families or even a gendered division of labor. What it does require is an unequal division of labor."[5] The promotion of heteronormativity, she argues, is a matter more of convenience than of necessity. Capitalism does not need homophobia to function, as D'Emilio would have it, because the acceptance of sexual identities has become a requirement of capitalism itself. Capitalism has managed to commodify and reify sexual identity itself. The collapse of the division of labor in the latter stages of capitalism's development has had a deep impact on gender relations, bringing about the end of the bourgeois family ideal of a father working in the community and a mother who tends to children and home.[6] Scientific and technological advancements (specifically the contraceptive pill) and cultural movements (such as different feminist waves) have contributed to a valorization of sexual pleasure by detaching it from its reproductive goals, thus undoing the traditional gendered-labor division. In short, the emancipation of pleasure has led to a total commodification of sexual identity. Lowe argues that this new sexuality has become "consumptuary,"[7] meaning it has become another good to be produced, marketed, and consumed.

The commodification of sexuality, broadly speaking, and of sexual identities, more specifically, has had important consequences for sexual politics and for those minorities that seek to overturn the destructive effects of late capitalism. For one, "sexual politics" seems to be trapped between the need to base its claims on some sort of identification and the awareness that a claimed sexual identity is the product of merchandising capitalism. In the previous chapter, I argued, with Hardt and Negri, that Empire has blurred the endemic division in Imperialism between inside and outside, substantially changing the way we theorize oppression and resistance. Writing about this collapse as it affects the configuration of sexuality, Lowe argues that the new sexual lifestyle, by "no longer respecting the outer/inner, the public/private oppositions . . . is subverting the opposition between heterosexual norm and its other, i.e., the so-called homosexual vice. We are verging toward polysexuality, i.e., sexual differences without stable identities."[8]

The sexualized body has become a commodity that floods the market. Thus, it not only becomes a product of desire, but also produces a sexualized subjectivity. The result is that the capitalist lifestyle is a sexual lifestyle in the sense that it has created a subjectivity based on the consumption of sexualized commodities.[9] Later, capitalism not only creates "sexual objects" for consumption, it also creates sexual subjects designed to desire those objects that will be produced. From this perspective, sexual identities are the last step in the creation of *homo economicus*. If, as Hardt and Negri have argued, late capitalism not only has erased the distinction between the public/private spheres, but has also, as Lowe convincingly shows, erased the distinction between the object/subject in the economic exchange, then a politics of resistance needs to look for sources where that dynamic is subverted, or at least, is resisted.

Sex and empire in the Bible

It is not easy to see in the Bible the connections between configurations of the sexual realm and the cultural effects of the political economy. To approach such a task, I take *porneia* as an entry point by which to survey the elusive connections between the macropolitical level of Empire and the micropolitical dimension of bodily practices. *Porneia* is a concept widely used in Greek, Latin, and Christian sources to convey the idea of "illicit sexual behavior." Since sexual practices are a defining aspect of a group's identity, *porneia* is categorized as a vice associated with other groups.[10] Accusing outsiders of *porneia* reinforces a certain idea of group identity and subjectivity – which has different nuances in different contexts, depending on how the terminology relates to males or females, citizens or slaves, customers or prostitutes.[11]

The Hebrew Bible uses *znh* as the root to convey the illegitimate sexual mores. Yet, as Phyllis Bird has argued, the concept is assigned exclusively to female subjects whose behavior is "shameful" or whom others perceive to have "fall[en] into sexual shame."[12] Hosea is credited with expanding the meaning of *porneia* to refer to idolatry (Hos 1:2; 4:12–13),[13] exploiting the connection between a woman who has fallen into disgrace and a nation that has turned her (note: never his) back on God. This connection allowed for an expansion of *porneia* in the New Testament in the sense that because anyone, male or female, can be idolatrous, anyone can fall for *porneia*. Interestingly, the Hebrew Bible does not condemn male prostitution (Gen 38:15; Josh 2:1; Judg 16:1). Certainly some warnings can be found in Prov 5:3 and 29:3, but, even here, no such condemnation is to be had. In the first instance, the reference is not to a prostitute, as such, but to a stranger who is an adulteress. In the second instance, the focus is on the economic aspect of visiting the brothel: He who spends time with prostitutes is likely to waste his wealth. The moralizing focus then is not on the male consumer of prostitution, but on the extravagant sexuality of the prostitute and the wastefulness of the services she offers.

Scholars have long noticed how the trope of the prostitute is oversaturated with meaning. Since sexuality is always an identity marker, the trope condenses anxieties about nation building. The history of prostitutes, suggests Mazo Karras, is not one of individual lives, but of larger social and discursive relations.[14] Postcolonial theory, both in literary studies and biblical studies, has analyzed the connections between colonial rule and women's bodies. It has noted that the anxiety about the other, on both sides of the colonizer/colonized divide, often gets mapped onto women's bodies. Postcolonial studies have been particularly helpful in unveiling the discursive relations between imperial/patriarchal rule and subversive/feminist responses.

In this chapter, I explore these connections by focusing on the image of the foreign harlot in the context of colonial rule in the Hebrew Bible; paying particular attention to the way in which the macropolitical arena influences the constitution of the harlot as an identity category. Babylon, as a foreign harlot, is a trope powerful in its implications because it is craftily built on a long tradition of biblical images, sexual innuendos, and colonial anxieties. Carolyn Sharp notes that "the prostitute as dramatic character provides an important metaphor for biblical writers interested in telling stories of risk, sin, exposure, the transgression of social boundaries, and accountability."[15]

The harlot is an especially rich dramatic figure when portrayed as an outsider – as a member of a different ethnic group – because such use enables one's identity (either personal or collective) to map anxieties onto the other. In the Hebrew Bible, the foreign harlot epitomizes the colonial threat to become like the other – triggering the colonized anxiety of being taken over, not only in territorial and cultural terms, but also in terms of desire. The figure of the harlot allows (male) authors to take their anxiety about female sexuality a step further.[16]

Since the feminine epitomizes sexuality, one could possibly argue that the image of the whore becomes the preferred placeholder to locate anxieties and regulations about the intimate life. Whereas femininity channels sexual anxiety, whoredom epitomizes sexual wreckage. This aspect is especially notable when the harlot is a foreign woman. The trope of alien whore condenses into political anxieties about gender (woman), nation building (alien status), and sexuality (harlot). In the following, I analyze Gomer (Hosea's wife), Jezebel, and Rahab as paradigmatic examples of such anxieties and the use of sexual stereotyping for collaborationist/anti-imperial purposes.

The sexual lives of Gomer

In her monograph on the root *znh* (harlot) in the Hebrew Bible, Irene Riegner concludes that the prophets, especially Hosea and Jeremiah, signal a shift in the meaning of the *lemma*. The prophets, Riegner argues, advance a notion of the prostitute as opposing a wide range of non-Yahwist religious practices, including saturating the word with inferences of "criminality, demeaning and humiliating female sexual imagery, and evil and destructive theological consequences into the normative non-Yahwist praxis of ancient Israel and Judah."[17] Accordingly, the prophets coin a notion of idolatry on the basis of illicit sexual relations.

The case of Hosea is exemplary in that he is commissioned to marry a prostitute to symbolize the plight of Israel. Decades prior to the demise of the Northern Kingdom, Hosea prophesied against foreign alliances and signaled this opposition through the prophetic act of marrying a harlot. In 4:12 Hosea makes explicit the connection between idolatry and harlotry by locating the "spirit of fornication" (*ruah zenunim*) as the root of Israel's deviation from Yahweh.[18]

Different meanings and their ideological implications

Scholars disagree on most aspects of the first three chapters of Hosea, and more specifically the disagreement affects our understanding of the status of Gomer. Some argue that she is an adulterous woman; others regard her as a prostitute.[19] Theresa Hornsby, for instance, interprets the metaphor as a description of God's desire to possess Israel. The prophet's actions reenact what God has done with Israel – portraying the nation as a former autonomous woman "who is finally compromised and controlled through the wealth of an outsider."[20] Hornsby concludes that the prophet is not a husband who desires the love of an adulterous wife, but a resentful client who desires a strong woman.[21]

Hornsby draws on Jon Berquist's hypothesis that Third Isaiah 55–66 represents the voice of the immigrants from the Exile who are invested in maintaining the status quo; while Hosea stands for the position of the natives more concerned with issues of justice and righteousness. Gomer is a whore because through this trope, Hosea conveys the idea that the nation (the whore) can be bought and persuaded to take an action that she would not do on her own initiative. Her revelry can be tamed through monetary exchange.

Yvonne Sherwood expands the notion that Gomer "needs" to be a prostitute to convey the idea that she can be tamed through monetary gifts. One of Hosea's merits, Sherwood contends, is to condense nationalism, patriarchy, and religious symbolism around the figure of Gomer, especially in 2:19 where God is depicted as taking away her words, thereby converting her into "a puppet of patriarchal rhetoric."[22] Sherwood further argues that, while at the conscious level the text allegorizes the religious life of Israel, at the unconscious level it allegorizes patriarchal control. The text's anxiety about women's autonomy responds to actual womanpower, an attempt at relegating culturally gendered elements that threaten patriarchal structure.[23] One strategy is to humiliate Gomer by creating the figure of the "undesired whore" who lacks the power of seduction and consequently, cannot be promiscuous because she has become unattractive. Such an approach evinces heterosexual desire and a male gaze for it makes Gomer a character at the junction of what patriarchy perceives and desires, not only in biblical times, but also in the contemporary world, leading some scholars to justify her doom.[24]

Accordingly, Gomer offers a glimpse of a woman prior to her colonization. The text's attempt at humiliating her creates the figure of the "undesired whore" who lacks the power of seduction, and consequently, cannot be promiscuous, leaving the contemporary interpreter powerless to offer a liberationist account. Sherwood seeks to destabilize the patriarchal ideology by showing how Gomer's presentation undoes some of her prominent features. Gomer is the main subject of the verbs "conceive," "give birth," "wean," and "to go." She "goes" after her lovers, making the woman the pursuer and man the pursued, *man* replacing *woman* as the object of desire. Sherwood argues that those positions are intolerable to patriarchy: Both female subject and male object are outlawed in patriarchal society because females are not supposed to desire and males cannot be the object of a desire.[25]

Hosea portrays Gomer as a woman whose desire needs to be contained. In Hosea 2:8–9 the author shares his plans to prevent his wife from expressing and acting on her desires:

> Therefore, I will hedge up her ways with thorns
> And I will build a wall against her

So that she cannot find her paths.
She shall pursue her lovers
But not overtake them
And she shall seek them
But shall not find them

The narrative reinforces the stereotypes of the harlot, by insisting on and playing up her desire and her overpowering sensuality. There is a similar connection in Song of Songs 5:2–7 between the construction of female desire and the material consequences of acting on it. In the Song, the woman seeks the man, but does not find him. Instead, as she wanders the streets in desire, she is found by the watchmen who beat her and wound her – stripping her naked. In Hosea, it is the husband who imprisons her so that her desire is contained. Such characterizations (as we see likewise in Revelation regarding the Great Whore of Babylon) feed on the notion of women as sources of desire who trigger male desire. In Hosea 2:13 the elimination of desire involves the elimination of all *jouissance*: gaiety, feasts, Sabbaths, and assemblies will be put to an end. However, as many commentators show, Gomer is a prostitute who does not stand for the nation.

The topos of the whore conveys, it seems, an idea of subjectivity designed to replicate/subvert imperial political structures. Unsurprisingly, the book of Hosea starts with a superscription that situates the writing between 750–24 BCE, between the last years of Jeroboam II kingdom (786–46) and just three years before the kingdom of Israel falls into Assyrian hands in 721. Israel, Gottwald argues, was under a native tributary mode of production that channeled its monetary resources towards foreign powers.[26]

Gale Yee offers four economic factors that situate Hosea's sexual metaphor within a macropolitical context. She argues that the metaphor of the harlot seeks to address the following crises: agricultural intensification, power instability in the royal court, religious conflict around polytheism, and agonistic economic interests among the power elites.[27] Yee's study skillfully connects sexual references to material realities by throwing into relief the connections between sexual imagery and native political resistance.

Yee, following Gottwald, explains Israel's economic reality as follows: The nation is focused on certain crops that allowed her to compete with other nations. The desire for "grain, wine, and oil" symbolizes the nation's promiscuity, its intent to go beyond Yahwist precepts. Israel's relationship with the surrounding empires exacted important economic burdens on its elite that they then passed on to a very impoverished peasantry. Hosea questions these policies through the term "promiscuity," establishing a link between a sexual image and the material consequences that being promiscuous had politically for those on the lowest tiers of the class pyramid. For the prophet, the solution is to return to a monolatry that reinforces Israel's religious boundaries. The plight for the masses was unbearable due to agricultural intensification, tied to a profitable foreign market and an aggressive foreign hegemony that insistently imposed its will upon Israelite internal affairs, and corrupt Israelite institutions of kingship, prophecy, and priesthood which oversaw this agribusiness, funneled profits to their own social sectors, and furthered the exploitation of the peasant classes.[28]

Hosea accuses the elite of betraying an origin, in which Israel was born out of a liberation movement, from an oppressive regime. Hosea establishes parallelisms between a wrecked tributary system and the national worship of the Baalim. In this view, the religious system mirrors the economic infrastructure. The trope of the harlot suits Hosea's prophetic critique, Yee argues, because it allows him to emasculate the male audience, especially the political elite. The libidinous wife allows her body to be penetrated by her clients in the same way the elite group is penetrated by foreign powers.[29] At the same time, the marriage metaphor suggests that the male elite has to make great effort to forgive the wife and that this is an example of what Yahweh is doing for her chosen people.

Yee acknowledges that the rhetorical move of identifying the object of shame with the prostitute reinforces gender stereotypes, underscoring the subordination of women in the marriage institution. However, a materialist reading argues that the metaphor hints not so much at the relationship between a divine husband and his sinful wife as the clash between the prophet and the male aristocracy. In this reading, the harlot is a trope to think with women about the nation. Yee concludes that the public stripping and shaming of the harlot symbolizes the humiliation of the nobility (2:3), her disgraced naked body coming to stand for God's punishment of the elite and their exploitative land-use projects.[30] In sum, marriage metaphorizes the covenant and the harlot codifies the political reality of an elite that dismisses/ignores the ethically grounded consequences of a covenantal economy.

Critical evaluation

Metaphors are uncontainable because the audience/interpreter can always open up new meanings and implications based on the symbolic nature of the language deployed. Teresa Hornsby has shown how in Hos 1–3 the harlot channels the voice of the natives against immigrants after the exile (whose voice is represented in Third Isaiah). Yvonne Sherwood focuses on those textual aspects of the metaphor that deconstruct the dominant voice within the narrative. Finally, Gale Yee argues convincingly that the harlot is a trope through which the prophet thinks about national exploitation of the elites implementing imperial policies.

These feminist interpreters' attempts to go beyond the literal/material meaning allow the reader to see uncommon connections between the theorization of the body and political resistance. The moralizing implications of sex outside the system are the perfect literal place to build on the condemnation of the nation. However, these interpretations, insightful as they are, do not address a fundamental question that van Dijk-Hemmes posed almost thirty years ago: "Why is Israel represented in the image of a faithless wife, a harlot, and not in the image of, e.g., a rapist, which would have been far more appropriate to Israel's misdeeds?"[31]

The sexual lives of Jezebel

In biblical literature, Jezebel epitomizes the "evil woman," creating a literary tradition that Revelation 2:20 summons in order to criticize the prophetess leader of the Church of Thyatira. In the Hebrew Bible, she is a woman, a foreigner, and although she is, technically speaking, no whore, she is charged with using her sexuality for wicked political ends. First Kings 16:29–31 narrates the marriage of King Ahab to Jezebel. The text frames the marriage alliance by portraying Ahab as a most wicked ruler in the history of Israel (16:30, 33) and as marrying Jezebel, daughter of Etbaal, King of the Sidonians (v.31). The immediate consequence is that the king commits idolatry by worshipping Baal – and the implication is that he does so because of Jezebel's influence.

The Deuteronomistic writer focuses on the worshipping of the foreign cult and blames Jezebel for remaining loyal to her old ways. She is accused of trying to kill Yahweh's prophets (1 Kings 18:4, 13), of supporting Baal's prophets (18:19), and of trying to avenge them when Elijah kills them (19:2). She is portrayed as an active agent who takes initiative and has political clout. When she takes the stage, Ahab disappears. Ahab, described as the worst king, is an absent figure (21:8). Jezebel, on the other hand, is an evil presence: She is the main agent in Naboth's vineyard acquisition ("I will give you the vineyard of Naboth the Jezreelite"; 21:7), spurring events that lead to the murder of the owner of the vineyard. The narrative makes clear that Ahab is Jezebel's puppet (21:25). Jezebel's sexualization happens right at the end of the narrative, when she makes use of her beauty to trick Jehu, portrayed as a Yahwist who seeks to restore the proper cult by overthrowing the Omride Dynasty in Israel. Second Kings 9:30 refers to Jezebel as painting her eyes, an action that is presumably understood as related to seduction and adultery (Jer 4:30; Ezek 23:40).

Jezebel embodies the warning of Deut 7:1–5 to the Israelites against mingling with foreign women.[32] Crowell situates Jezebel within a Deuteronomistic trend that understands women in the interstices of colonial rule following the pattern of what Bhabha has called "colonial mimicry." Here, Israel is mirroring the power structures of the empires that have conquered its land. The effect is the construction of an identity that fosters loyalty to Yahweh at the religious level and that posits Jerusalem as the political center. The murder of Jezebel represents the warranted prosecution of idolatry. The connection between idolatrous practices and sexual looseness is such that, although Jezebel is never charged with adultery or with sexual misconduct, she is assumed to be the wanton woman.[33] Likewise, in 2 Kgs

9:22 when Jehu mocks Joram, Ahab and Jezebel's son, the text mentions the "whoredoms and sorceries of your mother Jezebel."[34]

The power of Jezebel is also evident in the fact that she appears both as a leader of numerous court prophets who eat at her table (1 Kgs 18:19) and as chasing and killing the prophets of Yahweh (21:8). Furthermore, the text portrays her as looking out the window, which, from an iconographic point of view, has several meanings: that she is at the interstices of power, but also that she is the goddess of fertility.[35] Hairdo is usually a feature that is commented on to allude to sexual allure: women at the window are also famous for their "carefully coiffured hair, worked in the style that characterizes the Egyptian goddess Hathor, who elsewhere is associated with the goddess Asherah."[36] In fact, given the emphasis on linking Jezebel with Baal and Elijah/Israel's King Jehu with Yahweh, some authors have suggested that we are dealing with a war scenario between "god and goddess, Yahweh and Asherah, embodied in Jehu and Jezebel."[37]

Critical evaluation

In the same way that Gomer is portrayed as a harlot who needs to be contained so that the nation can be purified of its idolatry, Jezebel – who stands for idolatry – needs to be killed so that Israel can follow Yahweh and the proper religious order can be restored. If, as I have shown, Gomer functions as a "prophetic construct" devised to criticize a male elite that is catering to imperial hegemony, then Jezebel can be understood as a "Deuteronomistic puppet" designed to eradicate the perceived nefarious power of foreign cultural influence, whether religious or cultural.[38] Accordingly, Jezebel's character embodies nationalistic anxieties against foreign powers, and her death is meant to "expunge both queen and goddess from the text."[39] Jezebel has come to occupy, as the Merriam-Webster dictionary defines her, the place of the "impudent, shameless, or morally unrestrained woman." The question that the representation of Gomer raised in the previous section still applies to Jezebel: Why is undesired foreign influence portrayed in the image of a powerful woman and not, for example, in the image of a pitiless dictator or a power usurper?

The sexual lives of Rahab

Rahab is the paradigmatic example of the foreign prostitute. She stands as a symbol of political anxieties, her story of assimilation assuaging concerns about the incorporation of the foreigner into the nation. If, as I have just argued, Deuteronomistic historians usually portray foreign women as seductresses who tempt male powerful nationalist leaders into idolatry, Rahab – on the other side – stands as a hinge of the nation building itself: had she not eased the Israelites' conquest, the building of the nation would have been endangered. Where other "harlots" entice and seduce the faithful, Rahab is a condition of possibility for the faithful to prosper.

As the story goes in the book of Joshua, Israel is preparing to enter and conquer the land of Canaan. Joshua, the leader, sends two anonymous spies into the city of Jericho to scan the area and gather information in order to strategize the military attack. The two spies encounter a prostitute named Rahab who not only helps them escape when they are discovered but provides the means for them to break through the walls of Jericho. In return, she and her family will be spared from the killing (6:25). Rahab is portrayed as a deceitful woman, but, because such deception is carried out for the sake of Israel's salvation, the final appraisal of her is positive. The narrative gives numerous subtle, sometimes obscured, sexual innuendos. Once the spies arrive at her house they "lay down" (Josh 2:1; Gen 19:33–5); they "go in to" Rahab (Josh 2:3,4) as do the king's men (Gen 6:4; Judg 16:1); and the crimson cord could refer to the woman's lips (Cant 4:3).[40]

Rahab clearly stands as a metaphor of the land to conquer. Some interpreters have noticed how Rahab alludes to the root *Rēhôb*, which designates an open place. Without insisting on the etymology of the name, it ought to be noted that the open space or square refers not only to a site that is transited and inhabited by foreigners, but also to the place where prostitutes dwell (Prov 7:12). Since Rahab, very much like Gomer and Jezebel, is deployed as a trope to think about national interests, some authors call for hermeneutical practices that restore her identity markers beyond/before the whoring process. Vaka'uta talks, tongue in cheek, about the process of "Rahab-ilitation" to indicate the need

> to release Rahab (and her native sisters) from the violent gaze of the Deuteronomists' porno-tropic texts, and second, to rehabilitate the way we read in order to resist buying into the illusions of imperial imaginations (. . .) thereby avoid becoming porno-tropic readers.[41]

Porno-tropic writing manifests itself here at different levels, Vaka'uta argues. Once Canaan (identified with Rahab) is feminized, it is "readily spread to be penetrated and explored in the interests of YHWH's chosen."[42] The spies' occupation of Rahab's house presages the occupation of the land, at the same time that the brothel/house serves as a refuge against the persecution of Canaan's king.

In fact, the portrayal of Rahab as prostitute and the transactions involved in her trade can be interpreted as a metaphor of the transaction that happens to the land. As Rowlett puts it, "Rahab is a converted sex worker. She is a symbol of (among other things) the transformation of the land from sexually lascivious paganism (in Hebrew eyes) to colonized docility."[43] The connection here between prostitution and nation is even clearer than in the previous cases, for the liminality of Rahab clearly signals the liminality of the land and the identities that are about to collapse (Canaan/Israel). She is portrayed as an outsider who is incorporated into the Israelite nation in order to convey the idea that God (and the Israelites) has a right over the land.[44] Despite later attempts in the Jewish and Christian traditions to do away with her trade, nothing in the text moralizes Rahab's actions, making it easier for the contemporary interpreter to reappropriate the text in queer fashion. As McKinlay suggests, however, such an approach would imply condoning imperialism,[45] and underscores the need to work with conceptions of agency and subversion beyond the liberal paradigm. Trying to frame Rahab beyond the collaborationist/subversive dichotomy, Runions proposes the figure of the "trickster" as a label that situates always in-between.[46]

Critical evaluation

Rahab is one of the few prostitutes in the Hebrew Bible whose actions are not moralized. Her liminal identity is constructed to serve Israel as the occupying power. From this perspective, unlike Gomer and Jezebel, Rahab's representation as a prostitute fully matches its ideological function: Rahab's trade fits her role as a facilitator of land conquering. Precisely because the character matches the purpose, it is easier to see how in Judges an identity is constructed to convey an ideological purpose, or, to put it in the terms I introduced in this chapter, how a sexual "identity" is the result of a political and economic agenda.

Preliminary conclusion: whoring and the land

This preliminary analysis of Gomer, Jezebel, and Rahab as foreign sexualized women throws into relief the close connections between sexual stigmatization and nationalistic goals in the Hebrew Bible. The harlot embodies the dangers of being polluted, not only in individual terms, but also as a nation, showing to what extent the trope of harlotry stands for collaborationism, idolatry, impurity, effeminacy, betrayal, and so on. The link between the sexual immorality attributed to harlotry and nation building is remarkably explicit at different points. For example, Leviticus 19:29 warns against making daughters prostitutes so that "the land not become prostituted," and Exodus 34:15 forbids any covenant with the inhabitants of the land because "they prostitute themselves to their gods and sacrifice to their gods."

The sexualization of foreign women and the feminization of foreign lands is part of what Anne McClintock has defined as "porno-tropics," which refers to the European pattern of portraying white men as saviors of black women who have been, following the Eurocentric imperializing discourse, enslaved and subjected by black men. Women function, McClintock argues, as "boundary marker," transferring women of color from being objects of native men to objects of the imperial gaze.[47] Or, to say it with Spivak, white men's need to save brown women from brown men.[48]

One common element between the three women analyzed is their disordered desire. Desire is an essential category to describe the figure of the whore, because it is the vehicle that expresses her sexual incontinence.

A whore without desire is not a predator, but a victim, not a slut, but a slave. Sociological studies have long argued that the cultural honor/shame system attributed self-control to males and excessive nature to women.[49] This division not only pertains to gender roles but also to ethnic lines in the sense that Greco-Roman authors characterized foreigners/barbarians as effeminate and thus prone to all kind of sexual excesses.[50] It is not surprising then that the foreign harlot is saturated with meanings of uncontrollable desire for sex/power. Gomer is a particularly strong case in point here, because of the different layers of the marriage metaphor, the amount of details provided, and the varied levels of identification that the text facilitates.

In the eyes of traditional critics, Gomer is an adulterous/rebellious woman who needs to be contained by the prophet – in the same way that Israel is to be contained by Yahweh. Feminist scholars like Hornsby and Sherwood, on the other hand, see in Gomer an autonomous woman who is mistreated/misunderstood/misconstrued according to the androcentric values of the text and the context of the interpreters. Both strands of interpretation do, however, reify the gender binarism and assume (perhaps with the text) a straight orientation of desire. The reality, however, is that there are numerous elements within the text that allow for queer conceptualization of desire.

First, it should be noted that the election of a woman to refer to a political reality is intended as a shaming literary device. Describing Israel as a promiscuous woman effeminizes Israel in a negative way. To put it differently, Israel needs to man up. This is a strategy not unlike describing Rome as the Great Whore of Babylon. Although in Hosea there seems to be a redemptive possibility in the end, for John there is no hope for the enemy. The feminization of Israel through Gomer implies, on the other hand, that Gomer is masculinized. Such a queer approach to the image is built on a rather classic understanding of metaphor as a figure of speech transformative, not only of language, but of ideas.[51] Fontaine duly notices that critics usually feel "discomfort with the sexual activity reported,"[52] forgetting that Hosea marries Gomer precisely because she is a harlot. This gender instability logically translates into instability of desire. At a general level, destabilizing gender conventions puts the author, the text, and the audience at odds with "straight" orientations.[53] At a more specific level, Hosea's interpreters have noticed how the emasculation of Israel/Gomer affects the identity of Yahweh, the people, and Hosea himself. If Hosea/the husband asks the reader to identify with Gomer, then Israel/the audience is put in a position in which the husband contains her and seduces her. Hosea and the audience enter a sexual relationship, and the audience will know Yahweh (2:22).

Macwilliam, for instance, argues that in the prophets, the instability of gender leads to ambiguous "sexual identities,"[54] for, if women are men and men are women, such undoing of binaries actually brings a multi-directionality of desire across the board. Such ambiguity, Sherwood rushes to notice in deconstructive fashion, affects Hosea, who positions himself as an object and subject of desire at the same time: He accuses his wife/Israel of harlotry, but he also positions himself as part of Israel, which means that Hosea is split within himself.

These considerations throw into relief the different levels of representation/identification that are possible in the hermeneutical task. First, as already explained, the figure of Gomer as a harlot conveys the idea of a woman with unconstrained desire who needs to be reined in. I call this layer of meaning semantic, because the text activates and plays with the conventional meanings already linked to the figure of the harlot. In other words, at a textual level the trope of the whore already contains, almost tautologically, the idea of disordered desire.

Second, the prophetic gesture of marrying the harlot brings to the fore the dimension of representation on the part of the writer: The uncontrollable desire of Gomer stands in contrast with the properly ordered desire of Hosea, whose actions align with what is demanded from God. To put it differently, at the level of representation, the prophetic action underlines the differences between right and wrong ways of desiring.

Finally, in the third place, the trope of the whore (semantic level) and the prophetic action of marrying Gomer (representational meaning) activate/ trigger in the reader a trajectory of identification designed to align with the ideological aspects of the text. That is, the desire of the prophet to contain the excessive desire of the harlot initiates in the reader the desire to contain unrestrained desire. In the next section, I will analyze how this third level operates in the representation of the Great Whore of Babylon (ideological level).

The Whore of Babylon as a replication of the whores in the Hebrew Bible

Hosea 2 starts with God addressing his children and encouraging them to contend with their mother "for she is not my wife, and I am not her husband." Immediately afterwards, God calls to erase her harlotry signs from her face and her adultery from her breasts. God's actions are violent and remind Revelation's reader of a similar scenario: The harlot is to be exposed, taken to the desert to make herself like the desert, and be killed with thirst. (2:3). The same fate will be enacted on her children, because they are children of harlotry (2:4). Gomer functions as a metaphor of the "redeemable prostitute," the stubborn, powerful woman who can be brought to her reason by punishment and love. The metaphor functions by portraying Israel as a once independent woman who is now abused and doomed: once glorious, now condemned.

As I argued in Chapter 2, the Whore of Babylon is a powerful source of subject formation for the Christian community. The Great Whore, in this view, is a literary figure that channeled Christian disavowal of imperial formations, a means through which the communities construct disidentification technologies to counter political hegemony. In this section, building on some of the characteristics of the trope of the harlot in the Hebrew Bible, I will specify how such subject formation aims at shaping desire in the audience.

In Rev 18:9, John portrays the kings of the earth as committing acts of "porneia" and living in luxury because of Babylon and how they will mourn her when she is burnt. Scholars have long noticed the economic and political implications for the relationship between Empire and Christian communities of Chapters 17–18.[55] Accordingly, the image of the whore as a character of sexual trade fits the condemnation of economic trade inherent to Imperial Rome. If Gomer, in Yee's view, is a trope to criticize Israel's elite economic oppression of the land, Babylon fulfills the same role regarding Rome.

At the ideological level, John directs the audience towards rejoicing with the demise of Babylon. Chapter 18 starts with Babylon the fallen, explaining how she has become the "cage for every unclean spirit" (18:2). More importantly, in the description in 18:3 John explains how all the nations have been polluted by the "passion of her immorality," pointing at the kings and the merchants of the earth as being guilty for having been complicit with the "wealth of her sensuality" (See also 18:9).

Once the author has dwelled on the disordered desire of playing with the whore and partaking in her morals, the author portrays the voice from heaven addressing the believers: "Come out of her (my people)." The audience (both the original audience, and the contemporary interpreter) is summoned to redress their desire away from the whore. John portrays the merchants of the earth weeping and mourning, directing the interpreter towards a spectacle of rejoicing with the demise of Babylon. Desire cannot be addressed towards the whore because "all luxury and splendor have passed away and will never be found" (18:14.17.19). Desire is directed towards what is appealing, what can satisfy a longing for a need. Nothing in Babylon can grant a fulfillment of desire for "she has been laid waste" (18:19). At this point, desire is suspended and viable only through rejoicing in her demise (18:20). The frustrated desire toward the whore of the kings and merchants finds its resolution in 18:22–3, where the desire is annihilated: no more music will be performed and no craft will be found.

Scholars have studied the parallelisms between the demise of Babylon and Ezekiel's lamentation over Tyre. Specially, in 27:27–32 Ezekiel narrates the demise of Tyre, how it will sink into the sea and how the sailors will cry bitterly over its destruction. The luxury so lavishly described throughout Chapter 27 collapses, causing the mighty powers to mourn such an unforeseeable outcome (27:34). The extreme resemblances between the fates of Tyre and Babylon have led scholars, especially those particularly focused on historical concerns, to argue that Revelation 18 is a literary topos with hardly any real connection to the sociopolitical situation of first-century Asia Minor.[56]

Although I consider that Revelation 17–18, as well as the rest of the book, should be interpreted as a document addressing a real, historical, concrete socioeconomic situation triggered by the power dynamics of the Roman

Empire, my goal here is to explore a missing feature in most interpretations: The configuration of desire in the description of Babylon. Scholars emphasize the economic aspect of the trope of fornication, explaining how the sexual imagery conveys either religious or economical idolatry,[57] unfair commercial trade,[58] or the systematic evil economic structure of Empire.[59] Rome's main crime, as the consensus goes, is not any kind of sexual immorality, but its system of political alliances to benefit economically a political elite. The problem comes when the sexual imagery is interpreted as simply metaphorical,[60] as a superficial way of conveying a deeper meaning. The command to leave Rome is then interpreted exclusively as an injunction to stop participating in imperial economy or politics, not as a way to shape the audience's desires.

The ban on Rome is understood as a command to boycott imperial economic structures,[61] to invest an oppressed minority with religious and political agency in resisting Empire. One rhetorical effect of labeling the faithful as "my people" is that this situates the audience within the frame of the covenant. However, it is important to notice that by placing the people of God and, more importantly to my reading, any audience, at a distance, the rhetorical effect is that the interpreter looks at what is to come from a point of disidentification: The kings bemoaning the mighty city (18:9–10) and the merchants the wealthy city (18:11–17a) are subject to a spectacle in which the reader is to rejoice, displacing desire from their power sources onto what is to come. Even a materialistic reading that emphasizes the fact that John wants believers to see a condemnation of the luxury involved in the trade done by the merchants needs to acknowledge that the final goal is to shape the reader's attitude towards the erotic appeal of imperial luxury.[62]

When analyzing Chapter 18, scholars pay attention to the three laments – the lament of the kings (18:9–10), the lament of the merchants (18:11–17a), and the lament of the mariners (18:17b-20). In so doing, they look at the various nuances that allow for a different categorization of the groups' actions, positioning the three groups within the ranks of the Roman socioeconomic ladder. The kings of the earth have fornicated with her and have lived in luxury with her, but they keep themselves at a distance out of fear. It usually goes unnoticed that the kings are the ones that enjoy the most pleasurable experience with Babylon, but that their dirge is the less elaborated one. They experience the highest privilege with the least risk.[63] The merchants mourn the demise of Babylon for commercial reasons. Whereas the kings enjoyed the luxury of lying with the whore, the merchants mourn the economic consequences of her fall (18:11). The text dwells on the details of the merchandise (18:12–13), evaluates the whole luxury trade (18:14), and explains who (18:15) and for what reasons (18:16) the mourning is carried out.[64] Similar characteristics are found in the dirge of the mariners.[65]

It is not my intention to collapse all the distinctive groups mentioned in Chapter 18 into one class, but rather to point out their common disposition from the perspective of a theory of identification of desire.[66] One of the rhetorical goals of Chapter 18, along with the intention to portray and condemn the exploitative nature of Imperial trade, is to shape the audience's identification dispositions. To put it differently, the laments over the demise of Babylon aim at shaping the interpreter's affects toward imperial formations.[67] Such rhetorical effect is enhanced by the dualistic nature of the apocalyptic genre in general, and the specific images of Revelation in particular.[68]

Koester has addressed the rhetoric of dis/identification from the perspective of the slave trade, noticing how some traits are valued differently depending on what guarantees their legitimacy. For instance, whereas gold, pearls, and jewels are signs of a faithful bride if applied to Jerusalem, they are regarded as the whorish attire of Babylon. This double evaluation, Koester goes on, applies to the reality of slavery (6:15; 13:16; 19:18) in the sense that the reader can find a pattern where language of slavery (doulos) is employed positively to refer to those who are devoted to God (2:20; 19:2; 22:6).[69] Koester's main argument is that Revelation 18 offers an alternative value system by way of promoting alternative venues of political, economic, and social identifications.

Koester uses the example of a stele portraying the slave trade to illustrate how imperial identifications work (Aulus Caprilius Timothy). The stele is divided in four horizontal panels: the upper panels represent a successful businessman, and the lower panels picture how his wealth comes from wine and slave trading. As Koester describes the stele, the bottom panel shows a group of twelve slaves being sold, advancing the idea that "It is fine to seek wealth and status by trafficking in human beings."[70] Interestingly enough, Koester addresses contemporary concerns signaling the fact that modern interpreters would not understand the levels in the stele as congruent or, at least, ethically valuable.[71] As Koester argues, what makes Chapter 18 relevant and strong in terms of identification is the fact that John does not allow his readers/interpreters to identify at all with the allure of wealth, consistently reminding them that what makes wealth real is the blood of the slaves. To put it differently, whereas the stele under consideration guides the viewer from bottom to top so he rejoices in the outcome of slave trading, Chapter 18 guides the viewer from top to bottom so that the interpreter is reminded of the pernicious causes of imperial wealth.

Koester does not explicitly argue that Revelation 18 is a literary/textual counterargument to the existing inscriptional evidence, but he does imply that the stele is part of wider ideological apparatus through which slave owners aim at defining economic, political, and social relationships by way of showing how they have good relationships with Roman benefactors. On the other hand, in Revelation 18 such trade is under judgment by God. Revelation's argument agrees with the claim these slave owners make about their place on society, but John offers a blatant critique of the ethical consequences of their actions.[72] What Koester sees as work on John's part to reshape the commitments of the readers, I conceptualize as a successful attempt to shape a certain kind of desire that conflates economic commitments through affective ones. Pippin is right to point out here that Revelation works through a male-centered language that mirrors fantasies that dismiss any kind of feminine agency.[73] Although, as I shall argue in Chapter 4, John's economy of desire does assume a male reader and the unidirectionality of desire, contemporary interpreters (especially those following queer strategies) need not follow that script. From a historical perspective, however, it is important to notice that the imperial economic system unifies Roman and Christian sources in their configuration of sexual desires.

As argued in Chapter 2, Revelation projects the ideal image of the saints as an identification trope with important consequences for the configuration of subject formation. In Revelation 18, John continues this rhetoric of identification by calling for a displacement of desire from "within Empire" towards its outer limits. If contemporary capitalism has forged the straight family, one could possibly argue that Roman imperial economy has pushed the body towards celibacy – both underlining the masculinist assumptions behind that option and increasing the body as a tool of resistance. The propaganda of the *Pax Romana*, widely dispersed through cultural practices aimed at hiding the ideological underpinnings of its power structure,[74] is fully disclosed by Revelation with an invitation to leave the system behind in pursuit of a new economy of desire. The invitation to leave the system is not just a command to "come out" of the Babylon, but a process of building disidentification with her accomplices.

The authoritative role and the cultural influence of Scripture for contemporary communities lead interpreters to draw parallels between the context of Empire in the first century, and in contemporary times. As Callahan puts it, "John's art speaks to his world as it speaks to ours, for, in all the ways that truly matter, John's world of imperialist politics, global trade, and the murderous oppression of the poor is very much our own."[75] Callahan rushes to clarify that the identification is not based on a clear-cut identification of historical contexts but on analogical grounds; it is the oppression of empire, regardless of its specific economic, political or social differences, that grants hermeneutical parallelisms.[76]

I have argued in Chapter 2 that Revelation provides a unique resource to theorize an embodied theory of resistance, a starting point to envision new ways of subjectivity that counter the excessive elitism of Foucault's Greco-Roman sources and his obliviousness to the nefarious effect of Imperial formations on the all the bodies. Having argued for Revelation 17–18 as ethically relevant to our times, I want to point at the problematic nature of deploying its ethics of resistance without acknowledging the stigmatizing nature of its discourse – especially from the perspective of sexual ethics, and more specifically, from a theory of desire within a liberationist framework. From this point on, I take Moore and Glancy's reflections on Babylon as *porne* to think about how the anti-imperialist discourse is built on an imperialist conception of gender and sexuality that calls for deconstruction.[77]

John, according to these authors, deploys the cultural construct of *porne* because it fits his politics of contempt: It is the most degraded being in the scale of sexual ethics in terms of quality (she stands naked in the streets or in the brothel, not in the symposium) and quantity (her clients are few and anonymous).

After surveying how John seeks to invert the ideology of Empire by pointing at how wealth is built on the suffering of slave trading,[78] and calling for a disidentification from the ranks that profit from imperial economy, the contemporary interpreter must come to terms with the following question: How effective can a critique of Empire mounted on the very imperialist idea of the figure of *porne* as the lowest rank be? To put it differently, if John's account is a perspective on Empire "from below," it makes no sense that he would build his critique of Roman values on the further stigmatization of the weakest link: the low-class, diminished, associated with slaves, socially erased prostitute.[79]

John does not deploy the trope of the prostitute only as a superficial metaphor. He carefully unpacks cultural values associated with prostitution in order to make his anti-imperial claim more effective: she is tattooed, degraded, decked with the clothes that signal excessive desire, drunken, and universal in her whoredom. Moore and Glancy also point at the fact that despite all of these commonplaces, Babylon sits enthroned (Rev 17:1, 3, 9, 15). The paradox is resolved through the work of Sandra Joshel, who analyzed the figure of Messalina as the whore-empress. Joshel concludes that this figure channels the critique of excess of the female figure, regardless of her position in the social ranks.[80] It is these cultural features, Moore and Glancy conclude, that allow John to address an audience that would recognize:

"degradations to which enslaved brothel workers were subjected, including tattooed foreheads and perpetual vulnerability to violence. John's representation of a whore seated as empress is designed to indict the empire itself, and this representation gains resonance from its location in the wider pattern of sexual invective characteristic of Roman political discourse.[81]

It would not be accurate to think of the prostitute as a category of identity within Empire in the same way we conceive of sexual identities. We have seen that capitalism has created the "straight family" as the most effective unit of production, creating new sexual formations when production needs called for it. The figure of the prostitute however, I argue, hyperbolizes a gender system closely dependent on a political reality: power dominance is conceived of as masculine and submission as feminine.[82] The whore, with her ties to slavery, is the perfect embodiment of this system. Sex and Empire meet in the persona of the prostitute because she is raped/conquered by male superiority. What might be the hermeneutical outcome of positioning oneself outside a theory of desire that skips these male-centered, "heterosexual" assumptions?

Notes

1 John D'Emilio, "Capitalism and Sexual Identity," in *The Lesbian and Gay Studies Reader*, eds. Henry Abelove, Michèle Aina Barale, and David M. Halperin (New York: Routledge, 1993), 134.
2 Producing offspring was as necessary for survival as producing grain; ibid., 470.
3 Ibid., 473.
4 Ibid., 474.
5 Rosemary Hennessy, *Profit and Pleasure: Sexual Identities in Late Capitalism* (New York: Routledge, 2000), 105.
6 Donald M. Lowe, *The Body in Late-Capitalist USA* (Durham, NC: Duke University Press, 1995), 142.
7 Ibid., 131.
8 Ibid., 127.
9 Ibid., 135.
10 Jennifer Wright Knust, *Abandoned to Lust: Sexual Slander and Ancient Christianity* (New York: Columbia University Press, 2006), 51–2, 63–4.
11 Kyle Harper, "Porneia: The Making of a Christian Sexual Norm," *Journal of Biblical Literature* 131, no. 2 (2012): 363–83.
12 Phyllis Bird, "'To Play the Harlot': An Inquiry into an Old Testament Metaphor," in *Gender and Difference in Ancient Israel*, ed. Peggy Lynne Day (Minneapolis, MN: Fortress Press, 1989), 77.
13 "Prostitution in the Social World and the Religious Rhetoric of Ancient Israel," in *Prostitutes and Courtesans in the Ancient World*, eds. Christopher A. Faraone and Laura McClure (Madison: University of Wisconsin Press, 2006), 49–55.
14 Ruth Mazo Karras, *Common Women: Prostitution and Sexuality in Medieval England* (New York: Oxford University Press, 1996), 9.
15 Carolyn J. Sharp, *Irony and Meaning in the Hebrew Bible*, Indiana Studies in Biblical Literature (Bloomington: Indiana University Press, 2009), 84.
16 Marcella Althaus-Reid goes so far as to argue that there are no stories of prostitutes in the Bible. Instead, she affirms, "what we have are women identified as prostitutes, that is, whose identity is linked to prostitution even if this has been done for the most part in dubious ways (. . .) The prostitutes do not walk and we do not have theological insights or reflections coming from them. We do not have episodes taken from their daily lives (familiar or otherwise) and we do not know anything of their reflections about God and their societies (. . .) Their prostitution is part of the exegetical imagination of the biblical interpreters for instrumental theological purposes. In reality the focal point is seldom the so-called prostitute but rather an agenda of ideological issues which requires the use of the body of a prostitute to make a political or religious statement"; Marcella Althaus-Reid, *The Queer God* (London; New York: Routledge, 2003), 95.
17 Irene E. Riegner, *The Vanishing Hebrew Harlot: The Adventures of the Hebrew Stem Znh*, Studies in Biblical Literature (New York: Peter Lang, 2009), 203–4. Riegner goes so far as to argue that, for Hoseah, *znh* has no relation to prostitution or adultery and encompasses exclusively "a category of elements, rituals and deities, found in non-Yahwist traditions"; ibid., 122. In my view the problem with this interpretation is that it papers over the elements that make the metaphor efficient and striking.
18 The same expression is used in 2 Kings 9:22 by Jehu to refer to Jezebel.

19 Most scholars agree that Gomer is a paradigmatic example of a woman who stands for something else; Andrea Dworkin, *Pornography: Men Possessing Women* (New York: Putnam, 1981), 128.

20 Teresa J. Hornsby, "'Israel Has Become a Worthless Thing': Re-Reading Gomer in Hosea 1–3," *Journal for the Study of the Old Testament* no. 82 (1999): 115–28.

21 Ibid., 124.

22 Yvonne Sherwood, *The Prostitute and the Prophet: Hosea's Marriage in Literary- Theoretical Perspective* (Sheffield, UK: Sheffield Academic Press, 1996), 301.

23 Ken Stone makes the same argument in his queer commentary on Hosea: "The rhetorical strategies deployed by the book of Hosea rely to a very significant degree on the mobilization of male fears of emasculation, of being feminized," Ken Stone, "Lovers and Raisin Cakes: Food, Sex and Divine Insecurity in Hosea," in *Queer Commentary and the Hebrew Bible*, ed. Ken Stone (Sheffield, UK: Sheffield Academic Press, 2001), 130.

24 Brueggemann, for instance, notes that only one who has shared the experience of being humiliated by a harlotrous wife can relate to the text: "this is the faith of a giant of a sufferer, a man who had been through it, loving the unlovely, pursuing one who seemed not to want him, trusting himself to the untrustworthy"; Walter Brueggemann, *Tradition for Crisis: A Study in Hosea* (Richmond: John Knox Press, 1968), 108. See also Francis I. Andersen, and David Noel Freedman, *Hosea, a New Translation with Introduction and Commentary*, 1st ed. (New York: Doubleday, 1980), 249. Even feminist postcolonial interpreters seem to justify her destiny: Gale A. Yee, "'She Is Not My Wife and I Am Not Her Husband': A Materialist Analysis of Hosea 1–2," *Biblical Interpretation* 9, no. 4 (2001): 345–83.

25 Sherwood, *The Prostitute and the Prophet: Hosea's Marriage in Literary- Theoretical Perspective*, 311.

26 Norman K. Gottwald, "From Tribal Existence to Empire: The Socio-Historical Context for the Rise of the Hebrew Prophets," in *God and Capitalism: A Prophetic Critique of Market Economy*, eds. Norman K. Gottwald, J. Mark Thomas, and Vern Visick (Madison: A-R Editions, 1991), 17.

27 Yee, "'She Is Not My Wife and I Am Not Her Husband': A Materialist Analysis of Hosea 1–2,".

28 Ibid., 363.

29 Ibid., 369.

30 Ibid., 375.

31 Fokkelien van Dijk-Hemmes, "The Imagination of Power and the Power of Imagination: An Intertextual Analysis of Two Biblical Love Songs," *Journal for the Study of the Old Testament* no. 44 (1989): 75–88.

32 Bradley L. Crowell, "Good Girl, Bad Girl: Foreign Women of the Deuteronomistic History in Postcolonial Perspective," *Biblical Interpretation* 21, no. 1 (2013): 1–18. Following Irigaray, the author considers the possibility that Jezebel is performing femininity as a kind of masquerade.

33 Jezebel as a noun designates "an impudent, shameless, or morally unrestrained woman," Merriam-Webster (11th ed.).

34 Janet Howe Gaines, *Music in the Old Bones: Jezebel Through the Ages* (Carbondale: Southern Illinois University Press, 1999).

35 Nehama Aschkenasy, *Woman at the Window: Biblical Tales of Oppression and Escape* (Detroit: Wayne State University Press, 1998), 13–14.

36 Judith E. McKinlay, *Reframing Her: Biblical Women in Postcolonial Focus* (Sheffield, UK: Sheffield Phoenix Press, 2004), 88.

37 Else Kragelund Holt, "'. . . Urged on by His Wife Jezebel': A Literary Reading of 1 Kgs 18 in Context," *Scandinavian Journal of the Old Testament* 9, no. 1 (1995): 83–96.

38 As Wyatt pointedly notices: "Her foreign origin, her practices of foreign worship, her gender, and her exercise of poser intertwine to form a matrix of negative connotations. Jezebel is the other who penetrates Israel's nucleus of governance, threatening to usurp its identity by proposing that her way might be the better way," Stephanie Wyatt, "Jezebel, Elijah, and the Widow of Zarephath: A Ménage À Trois That Estranges the Holy and Makes the Holy the Strange," *Journal for the Study of the Old Testament* 36, no. 4 (2012): 435–58.

39 Janet S. Everhart, "Jezebel: Framed by Eunuchs?" *Catholic Biblical Quarterly* 72, no. 4 (2010): 688–98.

40 Crowell, "Good Girl, Bad Girl: Foreign Women of the Deuteronomistic History in Postcolonial Perspective," 7.

41 Nāsili Vaka'uta, "Border Crossing/Body Whoring: Rereading Rahab of Jericho with Native Women," in *Postcolonialism and the Hebrew Bible: The Next Step*, ed. Roland Boer (Atlanta: Society of Biblical Literature, 2013), 151–2.

42 Ibid.

43 Lori Rowlett, "Disney's Pocahontas and Joshua's Rahab in Postcolonial Perspective," in *Culture, Entertainment, and the Bible*, ed. George Aichele (Sheffield, UK: Sheffield Academic Press, 2000), 68.

44 John H. Stek, "Rahab of Canaan and Israel: The Meaning of Joshua 2," *Calvin Theological Journal* 37, no. 1 (2002): 28–48.

45 Judith E. McKinlay, "Rahab: A Hero/Ine?" *Biblical Interpretation* 7, no. 1 (1999): 44–57.

46 Erin Runions, "From Disgust to Humor: Rahab's Queer Affect," *Postscripts* 4, no. 1 (2008): 41–69.

47 Anne McClintock, *Imperial Leather: Race, Gender, and Sexuality in the Colonial Contest* (New York: Routledge, 1995).

48 Gayatri Chakravorty Spivak, "Can the Subaltern Speak?" in *Marxism and the Interpretation of Culture*, eds. Cary Nelson and Lawrence Grossberg (Urbana: University of Illinois Press, 1988), 297.

49 Jerome H. Neyrey, "Jesus, Gender, and the Gospel of Matthew," in *New Testament Masculinities* (Atlanta: Soc of Biblical Literature, 2003).

50 Davina C. Lopez, *Apostle to the Conquered: Reimagining Paul's Mission* (Minneapolis, MN: Fortress Press, 2008); Brittany E. Wilson, *Unmanly Men: Refigurations of Masculinity in Luke-Acts* (New York: Oxford University Press, 2015).

51 "If to call a man a wolf is to put him in a special light, we must not forget that the metaphor makes the wolf seem more human than he otherwise would," Max Black, "More About Metaphor," in *Metaphor and Thought*, ed. Andrew Ortony (Cambridge; New York: Cambridge University Press, 1979), 41. Regarding sexual violence in the biblical texts I fully endorse Cheryl Exum's argument that "sexual violence cannot be dismissed by claiming that is only 'metaphorical,' as if metaphor were some kind of container from which meaning can be extracted, or as if gender relations inscribed on a metaphorical level are somehow less problematic than on a literal level," J. Cheryl Exum, *Fragmented Women: Feminist (Sub)Versions of Biblical Narratives*, 1st ed. (Valley Forge: Trinity Press International, 1993), 119.

52 Carole R. Fontaine, "Response to 'Hosea'," in *A Feminist Companion to the Latter Prophets*, ed. Athalya Brenner (Sheffield, UK: Sheffield Academic Press, 1995).

53 Renita J. Weems, *Battered Love: Marriage, Sex, and Violence in the Hebrew Prophets* (Minneapolis, MN: Fortress Press, 1995), 80.

54 Stuart Macwilliam, *Queer Theory and the Prophetic Marriage Metaphor in the Hebrew Bible*, Bibleworld (Sheffield, UK; Oakville, CT: Equinox Pub., 2011), 48.

55 David Edward Aune, *Revelation*, vol 3 (Dallas: Word Books, 1997), 988–1010; Adela Yarbro Collins, *Crisis and Catharsis: The Power of the Apocalypse*, 1st ed. (Philadelphia: Westminster Press, 1984), 122–34; Richard Bauckham, *The Climax of Prophecy: Studies on the Book of Revelation* (Edinburgh: T&T Clark, 1993), 338–50; Elisabeth Schüssler Fiorenza, *Revelation: Vision of a Just World* (Minneapolis, MN: Fortress Press, 1991); Grant R. Osborne, *Revelation*, Baker Exegetical Commentary on the New Testament (Grand Rapids, MI: Baker Academic, 2002), 637–57.

56 Iain W. Provan, "Foul Spirits, Fornication and Finance: Revelation 18 from an Old Testament Perspective," *Journal for the Study of the New Testament* 64 (1996): 81–100. Also Stephen S. Smalley, *The Revelation to John: A Commentary on the Greek Text of the Apocalypse* (Downers Grove: InterVarsity Press, 2005), 451–65. This is the kind of position that Schüssler Fiorenza so vehemently criticizes for not taking into account the contextual force of any theological argument; Elisabeth Schüssler Fiorenza, *The Book of Revelation: Justice and Judgment*, 2nd ed. (Minneapolis, MN: Fortress Press, 1998).

57 See, for instance, Yarbro Collins, *Crisis and Catharsis: The Power of the Apocalypse*.

58 Aune, *Revelation*, 988.

59 Bauckham, *The Climax of Prophecy: Studies on the Book of Revelation*, 338–43; Schüssler Fiorenza, *Revelation: Vision of a Just World*, 100.

60 J. Ramsey Michaels, *Revelation* (Downers Grove: InterVarsity Press, 1997), 201–5.

61 Robert H. Mounce, *The Book of Revelation*, Rev. ed. (Grand Rapids, MI: W.B. Eerdmans, 1997), 321–5.

62 Robert M. Royalty, *The Streets of Heaven: The Ideology of Wealth in the Apocalypse of John* (Macon: Mercer University Press, 1998), 71.

63 G. K. Beale, *Revelation: A Commentary on the Greek Text*, The New International Greek Testament Commentary (Grand Rapids, MI: W. B. Eerdmans, 1998), 910.

64 Royalty, *The Streets of Heaven: The Ideology of Wealth in the Apocalypse of John*, 71.

65 Yarbro Collins, *Crisis and Catharsis: The Power of the Apocalypse*, 907; Osborne, *Revelation*, 652–4.

66 For instance, Bauckham signals how the pilots (18:17) mention their employers as the one bemoaning the demise of Babylon (18:19); Bauckham, *The Climax of Prophecy: Studies on the Book of Revelation*, 374.

67 As Koester argues, "Revelation's visionary rhetoric poses a challenge to see the world differently and to resist practices that are inconsistent with the faith," Craig R. Koester, "Roman Slave Trade and the Critique of Babylon in Revelation 18," *The Catholic Biblical Quarterly* 70, no. 4 (2008): 766–86.

68 God-Lamb/Satan-Beast, Jerusalem-Heaven/Babylon-Earth; Bride/Prostitute; Most notably, see Barbara R. Rossing, *The Choice Between Two Cities: Whore, Bride, and Empire in the Apocalypse* (Harrisburg: Trinity Press International, 1999). See also Richard Bauckham, *The Theology of the Book of Revelation* (Cambridge; New York: Cambridge University Press, 1993), 131–2.

69 Koester, "Roman Slave Trade and the Critique of Babylon in Revelation 18," 70.

70 Ibid., 775.

71 As I shall show in Chapter 4, I think Koester does not consider the subtle ways in which dominant ideologies affect contemporary strategies of reading.

72 Koester, "Roman Slave Trade and the Critique of Babylon in Revelation 18," 786.

73 Tina Pippin, *Death and Desire: The Rhetoric of Gender in the Apocalypse of John*, 1st ed. (Louisville: Westminster/John Knox Press, 1992), 92.

74 Bauckham, *The Climax of Prophecy: Studies on the Book of Revelation*, 374.

75 Allen Dwight Callahan, "Babylon Boycott: The Book of Revelation," *Interpretation* 63, no. 1 (2009): 48–54.

76 This is a common position in most liberationist readings; Pablo Richard, *Apocalypse: A People's Commentary on the Book of Revelation*, The Bible & Liberation Series (Maryknoll: Orbis Books, 1995), 173. José Comblin, "O Apocalipse De João E O Fim Do Mundo," *Estudos Biblicos* 59 (1998): 29–62; Dagoberto Fernández Ramírez, "The Judgment of God on the Multinationals: Revelation 18," in *Subversive Scriptures: Revolutionary Readings of the Christian Bible in Latin America*, ed. Leif Vaage (Valley Forge: Trinity Press International, 1990); Ricardo Foulkes, *El Apocalipsis De San Juan: Una Lectura Desde AméRica Latina* (Buenos Aires; Grand Rapids, MI: Nueva Creación; W.B. Eerdmans, 1989).

77 I have already summarized Moore and Glancy's main arguments in Chapter 2. Here I shall pay attention only to those aspects that are relevant in terms of the connection between Empire and identity, and assumptions about desire.

78 Koester, "Roman Slave Trade and the Critique of Babylon in Revelation 18."

79 Jennifer A. Glancy, and Stephen D. Moore, "How Typical a Roman Prostitute Is Revelation's 'Great Whore'?" *Journal of Biblical Literature* 130, no. 3 (2011): 551–69. The authors based their argument on Edward Cohen, "Free and Unfree Sexual Work: An Economic Analysis of Athenian Prostitution," in *Prostitutes and Courtesans in the Ancient World*, eds. Christopher A. Faraone and Laura McClure (Madison: University of Wisconsin Press, 2006).

80 Sandra R. Joshel, "Female Desire and the Discourse of Empire: Tacitus's Messalina," *Signs* 21, no. 1 (1995): 50–82.

81 Glancy and Moore, "How Typical a Roman Prostitute Is Revelation's 'Great Whore'?" 569.

82 Lopez, *Apostle to the Conquered: Reimagining Paul's Mission*.

4 Thinking sex with the whore in the present

Introduction

Revelation 17–18, I have argued in the previous chapters, appeals to Feminist, Postcolonial, and Queer Studies because of its use of a gendered, sexualized metaphor to describe a political/national reality. In addition, because Rev. 17–18 uniquely describes the relationship between a colonized minority and the workings of the Roman imperial order, I have used Chapters 2 and 3 as points of departure to analyze subject formation in the context of Empire and to reflect on the nature of the body as the mode of relationships affected by the formation of political and cultural realities. Whereas, in Chapter 2, I presented a Foucauldian approach to Babylon as a source for subject formation with emancipatory potential against Empire, in Chapter 3, I advanced the notion of Revelation 18 as a template to think about the intertwining of macropolitical formations (nation building) and sexual identities. I used the trope of the alien prostitute in the Hebrew Bible to explain how, by dis/identifying with her persona, the authors/audiences put forward an idea of political resistance. I concluded by pointing out the ways in which Revelation 18 calls the audience to despise Empire and its accolades.

Here I explore how I conceive of queer desires through "unhistoricism" as a historiographical style that bridges the gap between the biblical past and the interpretative present and that opens the hermeneutical task to a politics of desire that is not only gay but queer. My goal is, first, to set up a framework that foregrounds "queer desire." Second, I shall evaluate the work of renowned queer/feminist scholars from the perspective of a radical theory of queer desire. Finally, I shall suggest ways in which a politics of queer identification contribute to making Rev 17–18 part of the *Queer Bible*.[1]

Foregrounding a theory of queer desires; desire outside "sexual orientation"

Foucault theorized a transition, in the middle of the nineteenth century, from the aberration of the sodomite to the categorization of the homosexual as a species. This conceptualization of the emergence of this new specimen, mainly in medical and psychological discourse, rested on an innovative theory of power, known as biopower, whose ramifications have extended far beyond any discourse on sex, sexuality, or gender.[2] The now classical distinction between "acts" and "identities" – also used by homophobic biblical interpretation – derives from the Foucauldian argument made in *History of Sexuality* (vol. I) that, before the nineteenth century, homosexual activity designated a set of forbidden acts performed by males rather than certain types of individuals.[3] In the second volume, Foucault showed how homosexual activity in Greece constituted not sexual identity in itself, nor a core self, but a particular kind of practice related to the status of the self and the *polis*.

Closely following Foucault's work, David Halperin has clarified methodologically the relationships between history and "homosexuality," that is, *How to Do the History of Homosexuality?* Focusing on the study of classical Greece, Halperin problematizes universal claims about the virtual identifications between ancient and current sexual regimes, advancing instead a historiography that emphasizes the specificities of both systems in order to ban a trans-epochal view of sexuality. More specifically, he shows, on the one hand, that there was nothing "wrong" with the Ancient Greeks when it comes to sexuality[4] and, on the other, that "our system" has blinded our perceptions when it comes to approaching other "worlds," to the extent that we can hardly think beyond the supposable universality of our sexuality categories.[5]

This "discontinuous strategy" signals the multiple, potentially infinite, ways in which sexual desire has been configured throughout history. More important, such differentialism proves that "sexuality" is of modern invention;[6] it disidentifies Greco-Roman sexual-object choice from the contemporary sexual-orientation framework,[7] so the latter does not colonize the former but becomes destabilized by it.[8] The past becomes an estranged instance that has a queering effect on our universalizing assumptions of what sexuality is in general and what homosexuality is in particular.[9]

In the 1990s, Eve Kosofsky Segdwick expressed her awe at the fact that, of all the dimensions among which genital activity can be organized, the gender of the object choice became the dominant criterion at the turn of the twentieth century.[10] Sedgwick faults both Foucault and Halperin for trying to make a clear-cut distinction between the modern concept of "homosexuality" and the pre-modern notion of "sodomy." Such a supersessionist model, in which discourses follow each other chronologically, fails to account for the "definitional incoherence at the core of the modern notion of homosexuality," she says.[11] In axiom 1 of *Epistemology of the Closet*, Sedgwick suggests instead that we revert to "nonce taxonomies" or "the making and unmaking and remaking and redissolution of hundreds of old and new categorical meanings concerning all the kinds it may take to make up a world"[12] and suggests that "there is a large family of things we know and need to know about ourselves and each other with which we have (. . .)

so far created for ourselves almost no theoretical room to deal."[13] In effect, Sedgwick is concerned with the ways in which doing queer theory following a taxonomic model papers over marginal sexualities that have found no discursive place.[14]

Although Sedgwick only marginally concerned herself with historiography, her methodological insights have proven highly influential in queer theory because they offer a framework not only to study how multiple dissident sexualities have flourished at the margins of dominant discourses but also to interrogate to what extent "our normative present" ought to offer the lens through which we explore contemporary and past desires. To put it differently, queer historiography has grown to scrutinize the complicated ways in which past and present touch upon each other. From a "present-to-past" perspective, such developments are interested in queering the ways interpreters avow/disavow, dis/identify with, the past. From a "past-to-present" angle, theorists are concerned about how a reconstructed past provides the fulcrum from which modernity construes its identity. Both moves, I submit, are crucial in order to examine the "spots" that remain undertheorized in the back-and-forth between the present and the past. More specifically, regarding biblical and theological interpretation, queer historiography illuminates what remains obscured in contemporary debates about the "homosexual" in the present and in the past.

Taking her cue from Sedgwick's axiom, Madhavi Menon has recently proposed "unhistoricism" as what I would call a "historiographical style" to address the relationships between historical periodization and desire. Menon, convincingly in my view, criticizes both Foucault and Halperin for deploying a conception of history in which the diverse historical periods themselves determine erotic experiences. By ascribing varying sexual regimes to different ages, she contends, desire is organized in coherent systems that foreclose any variation of the sexual across time and space. Such versions of historicism are homophobic because they shut off difference. Instead of *heterohistory*, she proposes *homohistory* as the alternative, where desire is conceived as always exceeding any attempt to be categorized in terms of identity.[15]

Thus, unhistoricism problematizes the ways in which history takes the present as a clear-cut map from which to read the past and takes issue with the historicist assumption that desires are legible across time and space. Alternatively, *homohistory* explores the unpredictable ways in which desires always skip identity configurations[16] and dismisses taxonomies attempting to map sexual identifications.[17] As Menon puts it, "One can never know much about sexuality at all. Instead, desires exceed sexuality's capacity for capture; they flow, not only over the centuries, but also from label to label, complicating what we straightforwardly think of as hetero -and homosexuality."[18] Desire, in this apophatic fashion, resists being pigeonholed according to social spheres whether they are sexual (in the present) or preferential/aesthetical (in the past).[19]

Madhavi reads Foucault and Halperin's differentialism as providing fodder for a heterohistory insofar as the preference for "difference" relegates "sameness" to the background.[20] Her contribution exposes how differential historiographical models rest upon philosophical conceptions that work to occlude desires that remain at the margins. "Differentialism" claims to know how historical differences are configured and assumes that the present can be defined against a past that always remains "other." Menon convincingly shows that desire always keeps itself from being knowable and that our present remains as obscure as the past. In fact, "we moderns" can imagine inhabiting the present on the basis of our perceived incommensurability with the past.[21] In sum, "nonce taxonomies" are incorporated into historiography by way of problematizing any cross-historical and cultural determination of desire.

The "undecidability of desire" compromises both continuist and discontinuist accounts that stress, respectively, the familiarity and the strangeness of the past and sabotages any attempt to define the present in unambiguous terms. In sum, Madhavi exposes how the premodern[22] is the starting point that allows for a linear conception of history where sexual regimes are allocated following a curve of increased purity,[23] where chronology determines teleology and teleology governs desire.[24] In light of these theoretical insights, in what follows I retrieve Halperin's and Martin's versions of discontinuism and compare them with recent research on contemporary sexualities in order (1) to expand the unhistoricist framework by insisting on the undecidability of present desires and (2) to suggest some reasons why both differentialist and continuist accounts work rhetorically against a suitable theorization of queer practices.

From this point, I focus on unhistoricism's queering of the normative present and its effects on reading the past as a way to reassess discontinuist historiographies. For instance, Halperin needs to posit a clearly defined present where men of equal status take turns penetrating each other in order to establish a gap with the past. Here, picturing a clear-cut present offers the necessary fulcrum point to outline the differences between our contemporary middle-class male taste and ancient configurations of sexual desire: for the Greeks, male-male sex was exclusively acceptable in terms of status inequality, while for contemporary gay men, sameness typically defines desire in metropolitan middle-class sexual encounters.[25] In sum, homosexuality is defined by gender, pederasty by status. Halperin compares two different "social structurations of erotic life" in terms of a "history of discourses," but then slips into a description of current practices in a way that makes the present normative.[26]

It is certainly the case that contemporary gay identity is based on the person with whom one is having sex. Opting to read the past exclusively from this (mainstream) perspective, however, obviates the fact that many "straight" men do not care much about the gender of the person they are having sex with as long as certain protocols are observed, some of them not so alien to those of pederasty.[27] Here "gender" is only one variable among the many that govern desire, and in some cases not the most important one. For instance, many "white married men" find it sexually arousing to practice sex with twins: what is important for them is not so much whether the twins are boys or girls but their smoothness, frame, and lack of manly traits. Age/status differences set the standards of a good turn-on. "WMM" (White Married Males) do not self-identify as "homosexual," and, in fact, some of them experience their "bisexuality" as an enhancement of their (non-socially sanctioned) masculinity, which needs to remain on the "down low,"[28] thus proving the point that desire skips any attempt to be categorized under the homo/hetero divide.

The kind of historicism that "attempts to acknowledge the alterity of the past as well as the irreducible cultural and historical specificities of the present"[29] freezes the present and takes the oppressive discourse that it seeks to unsettle at face value. Picturing the past as *continuously discontinuous* with the present is plausible only if interpreters stick to the binary system "hetero/homo" and conceive it as a comprehensive account of every possible contemporary desire.[30] With its emphasis on presenting a radical gap between present and past identities, discontinuism essentializes the present in terms of the discourse it seeks to counter. Present sexual practices, behaviors, and identities can be better understood, I submit, if we read them according to "nonce taxonomies" rather than comprehensive and standards models of desire. Reading the past and the present in supersessionist terms hinders the examination of contemporary queer practices.

Our present time witnesses many "straights" having sex with other males for a variety of reasons, not all of which are "sexual" in nature.[31] These men are able to identify as "heterosexual" while having "homosexual sex" by framing their encounters in varying ways: those encounters are not "every day"; they are "accidental" or "recreational" (like playing a sport), as a way to escape a dull existence. Depersonalizing the sexual encounter by withholding emotional expressions allows these men to reaffirm their masculinity and, consequently within the dominant gender/sex system, their heterosexuality.[32] Empirical studies suggest that factual sexual practices have a conflicting relationship with normative sexual discourses. On the one hand, straight men are able to circumvent the "homo-hetero divide" that assigns exclusive sexual identities to individuals by way of detaching their experiences from the realm of the "sexual."[33] On the other hand, these practices demonstrate how inescapable the moralizing effects of dominant sexual regimes are. Although "sexual orientation" is the factor that governs identity (after all, the emphasis is on being "straight"), there is a significant gap between what the category of the "heterosexual" literally means and how it is performed in everyday life. This glitch makes this behavior really queer.

These and many other practices evidence that, in terms of desire, our present is as opaque as the past and resists a neat thematization under the framework of "sexual identity/sexual orientation." Although the overarching dominant discourse of sexual identity strives to subsume every erotic experience under its power and seeks to encompass the experiences of males and females who organize their desire exclusively around the gender axis, such categorization occludes desire's diversity and artificially lumps together the virtually infinite ways in which different persons organize their desires.[34] Therefore, I submit, the incapacity of the present to define itself in terms of desire destabilizes any attempt to read the past in discontinuous terms. In fact, Halperin and Martin are able to follow such strategy only by presenting the present in pristine, definable terms. Foregrounding "alteritism" and advocating for a historical gap between the classical and the contemporary period, Halperin argues that pederasty is conceptually different from homosexuality because reciprocity is what defines the latter: "reciprocal relations between adults and even persons of similar ages constitutes the norms for gay male relationships in most bourgeois societies today."[35]

My argument takes issue with the colonization that mainstream contemporary sexuality performs on present marginal practices and notes how such colonization is made the focal point in reading the past. Although "role swapping appears to be the norm in gay male relations today,"[36] and status equality might be the preferred option for bourgeois cosmopolitan men who identify as gay, I posit the following heuristic question: what are the advantages of taking "dominant sexual culture" as the hermeneutical lens from which different contemporary readers approach their dis/identifications with the past?

For many men, inequality – in terms of status, age, sexual self-identification, height, weight, body types, being out, etc. – defines desire. These experiences should not be read in light of the reciprocity that defines contemporary gay culture. As a matter of fact, new terms seek to capture the reality of proliferating desires in terms of inequality: daddies looking for sons, chasers looking for silver daddies, exec types for college jocks, straights for gays, fems for mascs, smooths for hairies, huskies for slims, blacks for Latinos, whites for Asians, straights for gays, white collars for blue collars, married for singles, bears for otters, and so on. Inequality is defined across multiple axes involving body types, races, ages, nationalities, wealth, professions, social status, body parts, or even sexual orientation. Here the partner's sex/gender is irrelevant as long as ritualized protocols of body types, erotic acts, and a focus on certain body parts are observed.[37]

These phenomena suggest the inadequacy of flagging "sexual orientation" as the exclusive and unique criterion that distinguishes "us" from "them." The impossibility of presenting "equality" as the privileged marker of contemporary sexual desires opens the door to new identifications with a past that is no longer entirely alien. The distance the discontinuist strategy seeks to implement is viable only if we take contemporary dominant sexual discourses at their face value. Given the complex morphologies of contemporary desires, why start with dominant culture in the first place? Why take the sexuality of professional males who penetrate each other in urban settings, share a household, and parade in the gay rallies every year as the measuring rod for the un/likeability of a dis/identification with the past/present? Why not start, rather, by looking through the lens of marginal sexualities not accounted for in mainstream culture in order to expand the epistemic/heuristic possibilities of the historiographical work?

From this alternative perspective, queer criticism is not only an analysis of the queer as opposed to the "normal" but also an examination of the gaps and ruptures that configure that which does not belong to the realm of the sexual. Paralleling Sedgwick's formula, queer criticism might here be taken to mean not criticism through the categories of queer analysis but criticism of them, "mapping of the fractal borderlines between [queer] and its others."[38] Such an approach is a performative act of debunking any attempt to normalize sexual desires, whether labeled as "hetero or homo."[39]

The alternative to discontinuism need not be a continuism à la Boswell,[40] but a more nuanced account of desires across axes of gender/identification/tastes/orientations that does not foreclose virtual dis/identifications with other times and spaces. If continuist historiographies unify desire across time and space, discontinuism unifies the erotic in synchronic chunks of time.[41] By proposing "desire" as that which cannot be accounted for in univocal terms, we can instead establish a relation with the past in terms of what Haraway calls "partial connections," envisioning a self "partial in all its guises, never finished, whole, simple there and original (. . .), always constructed and stitched together imperfectly, and therefore able to join with another, to see together without claiming to be another."[42] What our "joining" with the past will look like cannot be determined in advance and depends on the "self" performing the identification.

In a way, stressing the indeterminacy of possible political identifications with the past shapes this historiographical style as a Foucauldian project, because it does not discard the "oppositional potential even of grand narratives and continuist histories."[43] At the same time, it anchors future possible interpretations to a long tradition in biblical studies, a tradition that advocates a thorough contextualization of the flesh-and-blood reader, although such tradition has been slow and reluctant to contextualize the erotic.[44]

Revelation and desire: approaches within biblical studies

The implications of Revelation for a "Christian" education of desire were first explored from a rhetorical perspective by Adela Yarbro Collins in her groundbreaking *Crisis and Catharsis*.[45] The relief of the resolution to a perceived crisis is what triggers the emotional effect of Revelation, she argues. The reading/hearing of the narrative shakes off repressed fears while channeling them towards an integral solution. Gager, who provides the methodological basis for Yarbro Collins, had already argued that "the therapeutic value of myth and psychoanalysis lies in their unique ability to manipulate symbols and in so doing change reality."[46]

There is a significant strand of Revelation Studies that has remained attentive to the effect of the imagery on the configuration of desire, on the one hand, and the role of emotions/affects in the understanding of Revelation, on the other. One of the main insights of this literature is the evaluation of Revelation as a work that channels a crisis in the real world and offers a solution in the fictive world by way of channeling distress into hope. To put it differently, desire for Empire is turned into desire for the Lamb: the crisis caused by Empire is, at the experiential level, brought to an end through the cathartic process of building a new heavenly Empire. Three important scholars representative of Feminist, Queer/ Postcolonial, and Rhetorical-Emancipatory approaches have built their arguments on Revelation from this perspective. In the following section, I explore the main contribution of each, offer a critical approach from a queer perspective on desire, and, finally, lay the basis for a perspectival reading of Revelation 17–18 from the point of view of the undecidability of desire.

Feminist approaches: Revelation versus women's desires (Tina Pippin)

Tina Pippin famously spearheaded an interpretation of Revelation as a text against women's desires. The Apocalypse, she argues, is pierced through with the rhetoric of death and desire, "the concept of martyrdom and hope in God's utopian world,"[47] transforming desire as lack into desire as a tool for change. However, only men can use this tool for change, for there are no real women in the book's rich imaginary.

Pippin devotes Chapters 4 and 5 of her book to analyzing from a "gynocritical" perspective the sexual/textual politics of Revelation, and more specifically of Babylon. Chapter 4 is especially relevant to my purposes, because the author foregrounds her analysis of the figure of the Whore from the point of view of longing, teasing out the implications of the narrative for the right education of desire.[48] Desiring the Whore equals Death. Pippin famously asserts that desiring utopia overlooks gender oppression, an argument that shall frame the terms in which future scholarship will apply a Marxist-feminist lens to the Whore: the anti-imperial urge is built on the erasure of women's concerns.

For Pippin, Revelation 17–18 narrates the defeat of imperialism via the defeat of a desire that is annihilated in favor of a desire for the Bride. Such economy of desire assumes a male erotic tension that goes from male to female: "the erotic tension here points to the ultimate misogynist fantasy!"[49] In the following chapter, Pippin unpacks Revelation's misogyny by analyzing the way female desire is portrayed in the book (at the textual level) and how women's contemporary desires are obliterated by the Book's rhetoric (the "collective female."). Pippin's ultimate contribution is to show that females in Revelation are victims in the sense that they are the "object" of desire by way of stereotype: there are "archetypical images of the female rather than the embodiment of power and control over their own lives in the real or fantastic words."[50]

Pippin acknowledges that the gender hierarchy hinges upon straight desire,[51] which in turns builds the figure of the female body as desired and feared. Coming out of the whore and entering the Bride expresses a luring and strong sexual fantasy and turns "all the apocalyptic females" into "erotic images with erotic power over men."[52]

Feminist interpreters of Revelation have rightfully exposed the work of Revelation on the configuration of the audience's desire. Pippin notes Susan Winnett's observation that "the pleasure that the reader is expected to take in the text is the pleasure of the man" and she concludes that "a male myth of utopian desire has been created by men, and women who read the male myth are taught to read it as men."[53] Real desire of women is the subject of an altogether different utopia.

Critical evaluation

Pippin can be credited with being one of the first interpreters to address the topic of desire in Revelation in a comprehensive fashion: she pays attention to the thematization of desire in the composition and how the text shapes the audience's desire. More importantly, she pays close attention to contemporary understandings of desire in order to survey the political implications of Revelation's worldview to subject formation in the present.

As many critics have pointed out, Pippin's approach of "reading as woman" is dated, because it essentializes gender and equates all women's experiences as the same. Her lack of attention to differences within feminism inadvertently levels out all reading positions, resulting in what Schüssler Fiorenza has called "the ideology of the white lady."[54] To put it differently, any hermeneutical approach that departs from a contextual perspective needs to specify what location is being privileged, what idea of power is being applied, and what are the ethico-rhetorical implications of the interpretation proposed for the community addressed.

From the perspective of a theory of queer desire, Pippin's readings work only if we abide by the book's rhetorical dichotomization of gender and if we assume that contemporary readers do position themselves in an identitarian paradigm of desire. For instance, the archetype of the seductive whore luring men into porneia works only under the assumption that the audience shapes its desires according to heterosexuality. While it is the case that merchants, kings, and sailors are exclusively constructed as male and the audience is called to disidentify with their plight, a queer contextual approach complexifies this unidirectionality of desire by imagining those subjects as more than males and by imagining an audience as more/beyond heterosexuality. In other words, a queer theory of desire interrogates the text in ways beyond "reading as a straight fe/male.

Queer/postcolonial approaches: Revelation mocking (imperial) sexual desires (Stephen Moore)

Stephen Moore departs from a contextual approach to immerse the text in the seas of Postcolonial/Queer theory. He argues that the metaphor of Babylon builds on the imperial gender-sexual system, which is, in his view, meticulously replicated by John, who, in turn, pushes the system's inconsistencies to its limits. *Thea Roma* grounds an imperial cult focused on the strength of the city, always represented as enthroned upon the armies she has defeated.[55] Roma, on the one hand, embodies all the imperial ideals of masculinity: control, dominion, and virtus. On the other hand, and here lies the paradox, Roma is a woman, a gender associated with weakness, fluidity, and imperfection.

The ideal of strength of a whole Empire thus rests upon the shoulders of a representation of the weak gender. This paradox explains, in part, the fact that Roma is always "in arms." Moore argues that she "guards the sex-gender ideology of Rome"[56] – the achievement of masculinity through self-control and the overcoming of femininity through military discipline. John spots the anxiety about the fragile condition of masculinity on which the whole political system depends and exploits it to further a masculinization of (godly) Empire. To rephrase, John identifies the inconsistency of the imperial masculinist system and, on the same grounds, proposes a perfected version of it.

Roma, Moore argues, is a man (Imperium) dressed as a woman (Roma) dressed as a man (military features), that is, "Babylon would be Rome in triple drag."[57] Whereas Roma is, from the imperial side, dressed as the epitome of masculinity (a warrior), Babylon, from the colonized side, is dressed as the epitome of femininity (a whore). The trick, Moore concludes, is that, as much as Revelation's gender system plays with Emporium, it leaves the basics in place: a top male as an ideal over a bottom female. Roma (Babylon) is hyper-sexualized because social/national hierarchy is expressed through gender hierarchy: "phallic masculinity figured as female and clothed as virtuous and victorious warrior, then reclothed as a depraved and defeated prostitute."[58]

Critical evaluation

Similarly to Pippin's analysis, Moore's analysis evaluates the trope of Babylon as complicit with Empire. However, his analysis of gender performance shows a complexity and fluidity that are of the utmost importance to a queer contextual analysis. Moore's main accomplishment is to show how sexuality and Empire are closely intertwined in the figure of Babylon: she is a whore because Empire's political structures and morality are corrupted and vice versa. However, if Babylon's gender is overly fluid (from male to female and vice versa), it is not clear how desire on the part of the audience is going to work out. In other words, the undecidability of gender calls for undecidability of desire and, in turn, for the undecidability of interpretation.

Rhetorical-emancipatory approach: Revelation skips sexual desire (Elisabeth Schüssler Fiorenza)

Schüssler Fiorenza adopts a more flexible approach when evaluating the gendered-sexualized language of Revelation 17–18, because her methodology sharply distinguishes among different contexts (past and present) within an ethic-ideological framework attentive to contemporary contexts (an emancipatory project). Schüssler Fiorenza starts her approach to Revelation 17–18 by acknowledging that her own interpretation, like others that come under the scientific ethos, is perspectival. She also admits that one must account for the powerful negative impact of Revelation and its androcentric/kyriocentric (lord/master/father/husband/elite-male centered) language and symbolic universe.[59]

Two methodological insights are worth mentioning: the book is reality-generating and gender cannot be the exclusive lens of analysis.[60] Schüssler Fiorenza criticizes the work of feminist interpreters of Revelation, specifically Garrett and Pippin, for not differentiating between wo/men and the feminine as a trope, for stabilizing and naturalizing gender and not accounting for "the vacillation and ambiguity of a text that slips and slides between feminine and urban characterization, between masculine and beastly symbolization, between images of war and justice, violence and salvation, defeat and hope, ethical struggle and divine predestination."[61]

In Chapter 1, I presented and analyzed Schüssler Fiorenza's feminist reading of Babylon as a metaphor of a city (not a woman, versus those who essentialize gender) and her interpretation of the metaphor as anti-imperial (versus those who dichotomize the metaphors). Regarding the question of desire, Schüssler Fiorenza accuses feminist studies of studying *porneia/porneuein* exclusively in sexualized terms and shows how her rhetorical-political analysis analyses it as a conventional metaphor equivalent to idolatry,[62] which in turn is a critique of imperialism. For Schüssler Fiorenza, reading 17–18 in sexual terms means literalizing Revelation: *"not sex but power, wealth, and murder are the ingredients of Babylon/Rome's 'fornication.'"* The conventional use of "practicing immorality" as signifying idolatry she redefines as political "'intercourse' that negotiates wealth, power, and violent death."[63]

Critical evaluation

Schüssler Fiorenza's departure from "reading as a woman" rightly addresses the problem of gender/sex naturalization and pointedly skips the dangers of not analyzing multiple structures of oppression in intersectional fashion.[64] There are some tensions, however, that appear to be problematic when addressing Rev 17–18 from a queer perspective and, more specifically, when understanding Revelation from a non-hegemonic theory of desire.

First, Schüssler Fiorenza acknowledges that one must pay attention to the context both in the past and in the present. However, she essentializes the present context, foreclosing different approaches in the present, and assumes that past discourse touches upon a reality that can be, once again, transferred into the present. Although Schüssler Fiorenza repeatedly calls for a perspectival methodology both in her methodological and exegetical work,[65] she ends up offering a frame of interpretation that is unmovable. In the case under study here, to her mind Rev 17–18 only grants an interpretation in which Babylon equals Empire and John's response is uniquely anti-imperial. She further argues, in accordance with the theory of desire I am advancing here that "the linguisticality of all interpretation and historiography" implies the "undecidability of meaning and the pluralism of interpretive approaches."[66]

Second, the biblical text is for Schüssler Fiorenza a source for liberation understood as egalitarianism, a source for justice in the global polis. This project is problematic from a queer perspective, because it buries sexual justice under struggles for justice and because it does not specify what justice implies and how interpreters should advance it.[67] Schüssler Fiorenza assumes an earliest/essentialist Christianity that is egalitarian in nature and regulatory in scope, whereas my approach to desire makes it impossible (and unwarranted) to try to establish any link between text and reality whether in the past or in the present.

Lastly, Schüssler Fiorenza's ethical criteria are wom/en's equality, which assumes identitarian categories. If desire, as I claim, goes back and forth between space and time, not sticking to specific patterns, then it is impossible to foreclose in advance which perspective or identities will be shaped in the process, or how our allegiance as readers is going to play out in the interpretation of the text.[68]

Revelation serves as a template to evaluate the ethical relevance of Christianity for the present, how text overcomes kyriarchy in order to propel the interpreters towards a greater justice, offering "creative power which energizes and enables one to resist daily injustice and global exploitation."[69] From a Foucauldian approach, this conceptualization of power does not account for the multidirectionality of power and does not explain how resistance is always co-opted in the workings of power. To restate, there is no power outside of power which, when it comes to conceptualizing desire, means that it is no longer possible to distinguish the imbrication of desire and empire, the links between the sources and the goals of desire.

A queer contextual approach to Revelation 17–18

In the following section I relate my own contextual queer theory of desire to the theopolitical approach developed by Erin Runions. Whereas Adela

Yarbro Collins, Stephen Moore, and Elisabeth Schüssler Fiorenza approach the Whore of Babylon by taking textuality as their respective points of departure, Erin Runions has recently pursued the figure of Babylon using a different, although partially complementary, approach. She proposes an analysis of Babel/Babylon/the Antichrist as loci of inexhaustible cultural signification whose ideological import calls for new ethical engagements.

Revelation and desire: an approach from philosophy and theopolitcs

Runions talks about "apocalyptic desires" as an incoherent set of political allegiances and affections that brings together paradoxical realities: national law and exceptionalism, the heterosexualization of the nation and the homosexualization of the enemy. Whereas I am framing the debate around Revelation, empire, and sexuality within a theory of desire that seeks to skip the gap between the present and the past, the political and the sexual, Erin Runions has approached Babylon with similar ideological concerns but focusing on the philosophical frameworks that set the stage for debates about sovereignty and exceptionalism.[70]

Runions surveys Babylon as a complex locus that different political forces deployed inconsistently and contradictorily to justify hegemony and resistance. The ambiguity of the trope, she argues, lends itself to all kinds of political claims with important consequences to the realm of the personal and, more specifically, to questions of gender and sexuality. The ambiguity comes not only out of the polysemy of the word "Babylon" but also from the diverse textual loci that feature the city as central to their plot, which the interpretative tradition has conflated.[71]

After tracing the textual and cultural connections between the figures of Babylon and the Antichrist, Runions argues that the latter figure has been apocalyptically constructed for the imperialist agenda: from Hussein to bin Laden, the enemies of the state are constructed as antichrists and as gay.[72] Drawing on the work of Jasbir Puar[73] and Junaid Rana,[74] Runion explores the ways in which the enemy (especially the Muslim) is constructed as an effeminate figure that is disavowed through the masculinization of the nation-state. The ambiguity of the metaphor allows us to consider the enemy as residing within the nation and fostering a politics of fear due to the inability to locate accurately the source of danger. Furthermore, the "uniformity of apocalyptic desires"[75] foregrounds political initiatives that seek to fortify the law at the domestic level (attempts to ban gay marriage, for instance) while suspending it at the international level (Guantanamo, torture policies.)

Erin Runions continues her approach to "apocalyptic desires" by creating the expression "Babylonian desire" as "raw sex." Comparing this last expression to what Giorgio Agamben has called "bare life," Runions argues that the Babylon complex is able to host a series of sexual expressions that do not typically fall within the limits of the reproductive, monogamous, family-based, heteronormative sexuality. To use her words, "raw sex is sexual expression that is not justifiable within this (apocalyptic) teleological narrative,"[76] which shall be deemed to be the work of the Antichrist. This ambiguity, Erin Runions concludes, is what makes Babylon implode: the homosexualized Antichrist fosters the image of Empire as the savior of the world, whereas the inhuman Antichrist within questions that aspiration.[77]

Against the cultural value of Babylon as an ideological tool that shapes population via sexual regulation and aids a configuration of democracy serving the expansion of global capitalism, Erin Runions proposes the following alternative: a detranscendentalization of the Whore of Babylon/Antichrist as a queer figure that unsettles that transcendent ground for political decisions, "making room for the sublime singular encounter with the political other."[78] It is to this strategy that I now turn.

In the concluding chapter of her theoretical intervention on Babylon the Whore, Runions makes her most important contribution not only to an interpretation of the character per se but also to an ethics of biblical reading that takes the ideological effects of the text as a central concern.[79] Although her approach is hermeneutical,[80] Runions advocates for an epistemology of "queer opacity," placing value on impossibility, undecidability, the sublime, and the liminal. Spivak's "detranscendentalizing radical alterity" and "the impossible and singular ethical task of listening to the other" are the theoretical/ethical points of departure for Runions's analysis.

Spivak takes some of Immanuel Kant's insights on the sublime in order to analyze the ethical underpinnings of the sublime. After exposing the gendered/colonialist biases of the philosopher's conclusions, Spivak takes the sublime as the ethical challenge of impossibility, that is, the sublime points toward the radical challenge of listening to alterity. Because of this important task, detranscendentalizing is the process through which we stop seeing alterity as the place that can be grasped through calculation. The colonizing desire to know the other is turned on its head when we conceive of love as an ethical space that cannot be deciphered.

Runions explains that "once radical alterity has been detranscendentalized, a space is created to hear the actual other (as opposed to invoking the absolute other). It allows for careful listening to alterity and ironic interruption of the truths produced through subreption – without foreknowledge of the outcomes."[81] An important step in detranscendentalizing alterity is to consider the multiple meanings of the Antichrist by signaling the multifarious ways in which its invocation has ethical consequences: the Antichrist questions the ability to know – to know gender or sexuality, to know evil, or to know salvation when we see it.

Runions starts her analysis of the Whore by underscoring the need to look at the effects it produces: "fear and desire, hatred and attraction toward the Whore pulse through the text. The contradictory sets of affects produce conviction of her evil. The violence toward her is stronger because of censored desire for her. She is desired because she is powerful, wealthy, and sexually seductive."[82] She is hated because she combines desire and fear. Runions's contribution seeks to assuage "the cumulative theological effect of Babylonian interpretive fantasies"[83] by situating it within a decolonizing hermeneutical framework that explores the contradictions of those cumulative effects.

Her final move in the detranscendentalization of the Whore is to draw on the anti-social theories of desire posited by Lee Edelman[84] and Leo Bersani.[85] These authors conceive of desire as the epitome of an antisocial drive capable of staving off the constraints of identity. Queerness here is the difference that, like "raw sex" or "bare life," cannot be fully included into the social order, and it is precisely this exclusion that "must be tapped for its potential to disrupt the borders of inclusion."[86] For Runions the Whore represents that position, that element of the sublime that is beyond the symbolic order, because the undecidability of meaning opens an "abyss of representation," the place of not knowing and impossibility. In other words, the Whore occupies the place of unrepresentability and disrupts supposedly transcendental meanings such as the eschatological nation and compulsory heterosexuality. From this point, Runions takes up Tim Dean's exploration of hooking up practices to convey the idea that the meeting with the Whore can be "the place where impossible listening can take place, not based on intimacy, or conjoined identity, or futurity but rather liminality."[87]

Runions's approach is particularly close to my theoretical intervention because of her attentiveness to desire: Babylon is, in the end, a locus of love and hate, the affective variance starting in the text and continuing in the history of interpretation to our days. To rephrase, Babylon is "an affective theological force field."[88] Furthermore, her ideological impetus comes from a concern with contemporary *theopolitics*, especially with those cultural and political trends that draw on the biblical past in order to qualify what counts as a worthy life. Here the association of evil with Babylon/the Antichrist has the effect of situating the nuclear family within the state as the paragon of virtue, "backlit by the racialization and sexualization of non-normative families, ethnic groups, or nations under attack."[89] Runions argues that it is the undecidability around her power that "allows interpreters to insert their own desires and fears."[90] In sum, the detranscendentalization of the Whore as a metonymy of evil (and those identified with it) allows the possibility of a truly ethical encounter.

A contextual approach to Revelation from the perspectives of queer desires

Situating a theory of desire within the discipline of biblical studies

In the first part of the chapter, I offered a genealogy of queer desires in order to propose a theory of desire that is able to skip the gap between the biblical past and our troubling present. By proposing *unhistoricism* as the historiographical style to connect the dots between erotic experiences across time and space, my goal is to offer a theoretical framework for "queer biblical resistance." Interpreting Revelation 17–18 from this perspective means interrupting the unidirectional ways in which the text and interpretations of the text conceive of desire as going from one point "straight" to the next. Just to give a few examples: from Revelation's audience to the Whore, from the Whore to the kings, from the kings to the Whore, from the audience to the kings, and so forth. In the second section of this chapter, I surveyed how most relevant scholars in Revelation Studies approach the question of desire in order to show how, despite their theoretical commitment to contextual approaches and to the indeterminacy of meaning, they seem to ascribe to Revelation 17–18 transcendental/objective interpretations without paying attention to the book's actual readers.[91] Consequently, my proposal to read the biblical text from the perspective of queer desires is to be understood from within two turns in the discipline: the ethical and the contextual turns.

By ethical turn, first of all, I mean the paradigm shift within biblical studies spearheaded by Elizabeth Schüssler Fiorenza in which texts are analyzed in terms of what they do to those who submit to their "world of vision."[92] If texts, she argues, have been used for the purpose of exploitation, then biblical studies need to approach the reconstruction of the biblical worlds in terms of an ethical scale of values: "The responsibility of the biblical scholar (. . .) must (. . .) include the elucidation of the ethical consequences and political functions of biblical texts and their interpretations in their historical as well as in their contemporary contexts."[93] Although I have incorporated this approach from the beginning of my study, I want to briefly explain here its relationship to a queer contextual approach. The *impetus* to approach Revelation comes not so much out of objective interest in understanding its historical context but from a (queer) desire to understand how the biblical text affects the lives of the people in the present. Thus, the theory of desire I have sketched incorporates this ethical concern by offering a framework that takes queerness not just as a playful anti-identitarian game but as a set of insights that seeks to bring to the fore voices that remained unexplored/silenced.

Closely tied to the ethical turn is the contextual shift thoroughly theorized by Fernando Segovia. Whereas in Chapter 1 I argued that the ethical import of Revelation 17–18 cannot be fully grasped until interpreters pay closer attention to the present imperial context, in Chapter 2 I introduced the context of the present Empire as a way to evaluate Revelation's consequences for a politics of resistance, while in Chapter 3 I looked at the macropolitical and biopolitical critiques of such an intersection. Here I understand the theory of queer desire as a strategy to open up a space so that specific queer contexts and practices can be brought in. As such, unhistoricism provides a suitable complement to a queer contextual approach. Unhistoricism feeds contextualism by theorizing distinct and identifiable social configurations,[94] queer as they are, despite the fact that contextualism itself has been slow to theorize the queer.

Both the ethical and the contextual shifts coincide in Erin Runion's understanding of Babylon. Her *theopolitical* analysis seeks to understand the plight of the national and sexual other, and her reading strategies look for ways to deconstruct the binarisms (especially around good/evil) that ground those exclusions. Morever, as much as high theory as it delivers, Runions's hermeneutics takes as its point of departure the contemporary macropolitical context of US politics, from its construction of national identity by way of sexualizing the foreigner to its imperial politics by slandering the Muslim. Such a theoretically complex read is, in my opinion, a suitable point of departure for my queer contextual approach to Revelation 17–18.

The Great Whore from a queer contextual perspective: disrupting unidirectional desire in Revelation 17–18

Describing Babylon/Rome as "whore" points at her alluring and seductive nature. John describes her powerful influence by portraying her as controlling the multitudes and the beast (17:3, 9, 15), and describing her as a queen/empress (18:7). She is, on the one hand, invested with all the attributes of power, wealth, and luxury; on the other, she is stripped of all such attributes. This back-and-forth between power and weakness is what triggers the audience to desire/loath her. Revelation and its interpreters, as I have shown in the previous section, have a unidirectional conception of desire: the sexual terms that describe the ways the powerful interact with her (porneia) imply a male-female interaction on heteronormative grounds.

Scholars rightly point out the cultic dimensions of porneia. Revelation, commentators argue, does not refer to "literal immorality but figuratively to acceptance of the religious and idolatrous demands of the ungodly earthly order,"[95] portraying the alliance of political powers through the sexual metaphor of fornication (πορνείας αὐτῆς: 14:8). Rome is not only the political reality in which economic security is obtained (2:9. 13; 13:16–17); it also dwells on the temptation and the configuration of desire triggered in those who look at "it." In Rev 14:18, the second angel announces the fall of Babylon and defines her as the one who "entices" the nations to drink. The use of the drinking metaphor is on point here because the text conveys the idea that intoxication removes the desire to resist Empire. To put it differently, drunkenness eliminates the ability to skip a pernicious desire. Drunkenness induces spiritual blindness (Isa. 29: 9 and Hos 4:11–12). Such enticement, however, loses its grip when we consider desire outside the heteronormative national grid.

The allure that the current Empire poses to other nations, usually cast in sexual terms, can be disrupted when desire is thought of as going in different directions. The desire of a queer (male) immigrant, for instance, to participate in the indulgence of the economy of wealth can be theorized as a desire that bypasses the sexual aspects of the heteronormative framework described and is directed exclusively at the satisfaction of material needs. Queerness here calls to disidentify with the actions of the powerful (kings, merchant, slave traders) because of the *straight* ways they fornicate with Babylon.

Desire for Babylon is modeled by her capacity to bring economic prosperity to the nations. As seen in Chapter 3, this is a common trope in harlotry imagery in the Hebrew Bible.[96] Given her allure, John situates the scene in the desert (17:3), which is the symbolic place where one can be detached from the world's dangers (12:6, 13–17). As Morris puts it, the desert is the place where deception can be avoided.[97] The text does emphasize that John "marvels" at the vision of the beast and the woman, thus suggesting the voyeuristic disposition of the author/audience. This going back and forth between admiration and rejection is designed, as many authors suggest, to shape the desire of the audience/readers.[98] The ambiguity between attraction/rejection is further emphasized in 17:4, where the woman is heavily adorned, whereas in her hands she holds the deeds of her harlotry (see also the contrast in 18:16). Once again, the reference to the cup implies that she needs to intoxicate her followers in order to seduce them, restating the link between physical attractiveness and the allure of wealth.

Once again, when desire skips the constraints of unidirectionality, the reader responds to the allure of the Whore and to the reaction of the crowds to the Whore in different ways. The queer reader might disrupt the assumed attraction that the Whore poses: her features are not appealing in a sexual way. Furthermore, queer desire might put the reader in a position to occupy the place of the Whore. The Whore, to follow Moore's argument, is in drag and, consequently, the interpreter might not want to disidentify with her but to "be her."

After describing Babylon's political clout in sexual terms, 17:5 equates both dimensions in superlative terms, preparing the audience for the introduction of the bride of Christ.[99] At the same time, the Whore is drunk herself (17:7), underscoring the fact that being drunk is a metaphor for the excess of indulging in her proposal. It is worth noticing that Revelation repeatedly uses the verb "marvel at" (θαυμάζω; 13:3; 17:6, 7, 8) to convey the idea that John/the audience is enticed by the woman/beast's allure.[100] In 17:8 the voyeuristic aspect of worshipping the beast is conveyed through the use of the verb βλέπω, but this time the subject is those whose names "have not been written in the book of life from the foundation of the world," in contraposition to those whose names are written in the book.

Not surprisingly, the disavowal of desire for political clout and the shaping of desire away for sexual desire are promoted through the design of a time frame where the end is around the corner. John tells the churches that they ought to expect "the end" really soon and that the reward for their sacrifice is imminent. Education of desire is achieved here through the apocalyptic framework, whereby future and present collapse (17:10).[101] Accordingly, John portrays the enemy as a reality that "was" but "no longer is."

In 17:16, John narrates how the "ten horns" and the "beast" turn against the harlot, make her desolate and naked, and set her on fire. This is all the more striking because in 18:9–10 the kings and the multitudes mourn over the destruction. Scholars seek to resolve this paradox in one of two ways: by arguing that both passages refer to different constituencies, thus setting up a chronological framework in which the conspirers mourn her demise because they realize (too late) that they will vanish with her; or by hypothesizing that the political powers (kings) turn against the idolatrous religious system.[102] Although these explanations are reasonable, they seek to do away with the intrinsic nature of Revelation as a riddle that cannot be expressed in propositions but can be contemplated/experienced only through its imagery. From the perspective of desire, the paradox is easily explained: what one desires now may turn into what one despises later. So when she is portrayed as the woman who reigns over the kings (17:18) but is destroyed by her, John is inviting the audience to imagine a desire split against itself, illustrating – through the demise of the object of desire – that identification with the whore shall irremediably turn into desolation.

Chapter 18 starts with the acknowledgment of the power of the heavenly court, for the angel who is about to announce the fall of Babylon the Great (18:2) is invested with authority (ἔχοντα ἐξουσίαν)[103] and the earth is illuminated by his glory (δόξα), a term that serves to describe the power, splendor, and triumph of the heavenly realm and the New Jerusalem (19:1, 7; 21:11, 24, 24, 26). The contrast between the glorious appearance and the loud voice of the representative of heaven and the announcement of Babylon's fall induces the audience to shift allegiance to the army of the Lamb. Rev 18:2 alludes to Isa 21:9, where "fallen, fallen is Babylon" is followed by "all the images of her gods are shattered on the ground." In other words, any desire/admiration for her attributes no longer makes sense because she is gone.

This scene of destruction prepares a recapitulation of what happens to those who have desired Babylon, so that "we" do not make the same mistake. As many commentators have noticed, "drinking her wine" and "fornicating with her" do not represent literal immorality but "a figurative depiction of acceptance of Babylon's religious and idolatrous demands."[104] What these interpretations miss, however, is that John's rhetoric seeks to model his audience's desire on the grounds of sexual drives. Those demands might lose their appeal for queer male readers for whom indulging in the excess of sex with a female is not an option. Conversely, for queer female readers, fulfilling those desires might mean participating in occasional erotic experiences without fulfilling the requirements of porneia.

The injunction to "come out of her" in 18:4 is, as elaborated in Chapter 3, a call to disidentify with the *theopolitics* of Empire, to use Runions's expression. The verse echoes Isa 52:11, where the prophet exhorts his audience to remain away from the unclean, and Jer 51:45, where the prophet exhorts Israel to depart from Babylon's idolatry. The difference here is that the emphasis on the sexual nature of desire lies at the basis of the rejection of the political critique. For instance, the term στρηνιάω describes the life of excess in which she indulged (18:7), enticing the kings to follow along (18:9).[105] Excess includes, as scholars point out, wealth and political power but also the excesses of uncontrolled desire,[106] which, as Stephen Moore has pointedly argued, results in the emasculation of the Roman elite.[107] What is particularly relevant here is that the consequence of indulging in that desire brings "weeping" and "mourning." The link between the "love of excess," "plagues," "inordinate desire," and "weeping and mourning" is all too familiar to members of the queer community who have gone through the AIDS crisis. For them, Babylon is a reminder of the lives taken and of the slander still directed towards those who have participated in "that excess." The queer reader is resistant to leave, "to come out of her," because that would mean leaving a history of loss behind.

The call to abandon desire for the Whore is not only implemented through the urgency implied by the apocalyptic timeframe but also through an invitation to shift one kind of excess for another. Revelation 18:16 describes the harlot/city in a way that stands in opposition to the Christ's pure bride/city (21:1, 10–23). However, as expected, desire for the luxury of the Bride is not condemned nor does it result in death. The one "adorned with every kind of precious stone" and "gold" takes up all desire left from those who might have desired but did not go "all the way through."[108] To put it differently, the reward of those who have been able to contain desire is the rejoicing over the fall of those who have let their desires go astray (18:20). But since queer desire has been going in all different directions, we can no longer identify who is rejoicing and who is mourning.

Notes

1 Ken Stone, *Queer Commentary and the Hebrew Bible*, Journal for the Study of the Old Testament. Supplement Series 334 (Cleveland, OH: Pilgrim Press, 2001); Deryn Guest, Robert E. Goss, Mona West, and Thomas Bohache, *The Queer Bible Commentary* (London: SCM, 2006). Stephen D. Moore, and ebrary Inc., *God's Beauty Parlor and Other Queer Spaces in and Around the Bible* (Stanford, CA: Stanford University Press, 2001), http://site.ebrary.com/lib/yale/Doc?id=10042833. Teresa J. Hornsby, and Ken Stone, *Bible Trouble Queer Reading at the Boundaries of Biblical Scholarship* (Atlanta: Society of Biblical Literature, 2011).

2 For an analysis of the methodological consequences of taking seriously the capillary nature of power, see Barry Smart, *Michel Foucault* (London; New York: E. Horwood; Tavistock Publications, 1985), 79. The importance of Foucault's conception of power for queer politics and activism can hardly be underestimated. The "queer movement" mined this definition of power in order to fight a homophobia that was reconceptualized not as a hatred coming (only) from the state or the law but as a discourse that saturated the entire field of cultural and social

representation, a set of not necessarily rational forces that pervaded processes of socialization, subjectivation, and objectification. See David M. Halperin, *Saint Foucault: Towards a Gay Hagiography* (New York: Oxford University Press, 1995).

3 Yet Foucault posited different points of origin for "homosexuality" in different works (see Didier Eribon, "Michel Foucault's Histories of Sexuality," *GLQ: A Journal of Lesbian and Gay Studies* 7, no. 1 (2001): 31–86. Furthermore, the now classical distinction between "acts" and "identities," as Foucauldian scholarship has shown, has been affixed to *History of Sexuality* (vol. 1) by later debate (see Lynne Huffer, *Mad for Foucault: Rethinking the Foundations of Queer Theory* (New York: Columbia University Press, 2010), 67–82.

4 David M. Halperin, *How to Do the History of Homosexuality* (Chicago: University of Chicago Press, 2002), 3.

5 Ibid.

6 Halperin sets out to "denaturalize the sexual body by historicizing it, by illuminating its multiple determinations in historical culture, in so doing to contest the body's use as a site for the production of heterosexual meanings and for their transformation into timeless and universal realities," ibid., 84.

7 Halperin considers that for "us," inheritors of the Kinsey scale, it is impossible to think of sexual preference outside sexual orientation, of sexual choices without falling back on to "sexuality"; ibid., 91. As will become clear in the next section, I problematize assumptions about the "us"

8 Halperin seeks a reading of the Erotes that balances his cultural specificity – by carefully setting aside potential colonizations of "our" system – and his relevance for contemporary queer politics. Although Halperin achieves the first goal, the second one remains to be fully developed.

9 The ultimate effect "will be to defamiliarize current sexual behaviors and attitudes and to destabilize the binary opposition between heterosexuality and homosexuality that so decisively structures contemporary discourses of homophobia". Halperin, *How to Do the History of Homosexuality*, 92. The problem, I contend, is that by choosing to read the past from the dominant homo/hetero divide, Halperin performatively reaffirms it.

10 Eve Kosofsky Sedgwick, *Epistemology of the Closet* (New York; London: Harvester Wheatsheaf, 1991), 8.

11 Halperin, *How to Do the History of Homosexuality*, 12.

12 Sedgwick, *Epistemology of the Closet*, 23.

13 Ibid., 24.

14 Given the relevance of Sedgwick's contribution to my argument, I quote her here at length. She notices the following differences: "To some, the focus of 'the sexual' seems scarcely to extend beyond the boundaries of discrete genital acts; to others, it enfolds them loosely or floats virtually free of them. Even identical genital acts mean different things to different people. Sexuality makes up a large share of the self-perceived identity of some, a small share of others. Some spend a lot of time thinking about sex, others little. Some people like to have a lot of sex, others little or none. Many people have their richest mental/emotional involvement with sexual acts that they don't do, or even don't want to do. For some people, it is important that sex be embedded in contexts resonant with meaning, narrative, and connectedness with other aspects of their life; for other people, it is important that they not be; to others, it doesn't occur that they might be. For some people, particular sexual preferences are so fixed in memory and durable that they can only be seen as innate; for others, they appear to arise later or feel discretionary. For some people, the possibility of bad sex is aversive enough that their lives are strongly marked by its avoidance; for others, it isn't. For some people, their sexuality provides a needed space of heightened discovery

and cognitive hyperstimulation. For others, sexuality provides a needed space for routinized habituation and cognitive hiatus. Some people like spontaneous sexual scenes, others like highly scripted ones, others like spontaneous-sounding ones that are nonetheless totally predictable. Some people's sexuality is intensely marked by autoerotic pleasures and histories. For others, this possibility seems secondary or fragile, if it exists at all. Some people, regardless of orientation, experience their sexuality as deeply embedded in a matrix of gender and all that entails. Others do not. These differentiations can occur not just between people, but within the same person during different periods," ibid., 25–6.

15 Madhavi Menon, *Unhistorical Shakespeare: Queer Theory in Shakespearean Literature and Film*, 1st ed. (New York: Palgrave Macmillan, 2008), 2.

16 Ibid., 3.

17 Ibid., 5. In the same way, Bersani argues that "the mobility of desires defeats the project of fixing identity by way of a science of desires"; Leo Bersani, *Homos* (Cambridge, MA: Harvard University Press, 1995), 107.

18 Menon, *Unhistorical Shakespeare: Queer Theory in Shakespearean Literature and Film*, 5.

19 By preferential, I refer here to Foucault and Halperin's argument that desire cannot be linked to the sexual in the past (as a mode of subjectivity from which identity is attained).

20 I disagree with Menon on this point as one can underscore sameness and still produce homophobic homohistory. In the same vein, the author seems to conflate a history of discourses and a history of practices when she blames differentialism for not paying attention to the unpredictable ways in which desire shows up and cannot be thematized.

21 Or, as Freccero and Fradenburg put it: "We are modern insofar as we know that we are incommensurably different form our past and from other cultures. A culture that can think its radical difference, eschewing providential, universalist, or evolutionary narratives of human time – this is modernity"; L. O. Aranye Fradenburg, and Carla Freccero, *Premodern Sexualities* (New York: Routledge, 1995), xxv. Later they formulate the following challenging question: "Is it not the case that alteritism at times functions precisely to stabilize the identity of 'the modern'?" Ibid., xix.

22 Although Madhavi focuses on Shakespeare's period, her insights are applicable to the biblical past.

23 Menon, *Unhistorical Shakespeare*, 18.

24 Ibid., 19. Such critique does not apply exclusively to studies of desire across time but also across space. Much of contemporary queer anthropology on diaspora and alien sexualities relies on the category of the "different" in order to pursue aboriginal concepts detached from "our time and space." These strategies not only can be accused of orientalism but work to keep "our" time and space consistently "normal" and unexamined. For an illustration of such "otherization" see the otherwise excellent study by Don Kulick, *Travesti: Sex, Gender, and Culture Among Brazilian Transgendered Prostitutes*, Worlds of Desire (Chicago: University of Chicago Press, 1998).

25 Comparing the present and the past, Halperin argues that, for the Erotes, desire is grounded on status inequality. Any sexual appeal between two adult men is unconceivable. Halperin, *How to Do the History of Homosexuality*, 94. The text, he argues, goes out of its way to clarify who would count as the *eromenos* and as the *erotes* in the relationship: signs of facial or body hair, muscle development . . . are the features to be accounted for in order to make clear that sex among males can take place only in terms of status inequality.

26 Halperin insists that one of the differences that grants discontinuity is "the text's emphasis on pederasty to the exclusion of homosexuality (whose existence, apparently, is not even recognized," ibid., 99.

27 See, for instance, the evidence showing that non-identified males who have sex with other males tend to play the insertive role as a way to protect their masculinity; Karolynn Siegel, Eric W. Schrimshaw, Helen-Maria Lekas, and Jeffrey T. Parsons, "Sexual Behaviors of Non-Gay Identified Non-Disclosing Men Who Have Sex with Men and Women," *Archives of Sexual Behavior* 37, no. 5 (2008): 732–34.

28 Studies on the "down low" are lacking from a queer perspective. I have not found any scholarly study on the sexual taxonomies that take into account 'Craigslist' sexuality. Some non-scholarly documented examples can be found in Keith Boykin, *Beyond the Down Low: Sex and Denial in Black America* (New York: Carroll & Graf, 2005), 8–11. Boykin contests media definitions of the down low to show the conflicting ways in which down low, on the one hand, and gay and homosexual, on the other, do not overlap. The emphasis on understanding all sexual identities along the lines of the hetero/homo divide leads many studies to tackle the issue of the down low as self-denial or misperception of the sexual self: "Individuals who are on the down low avoid incorporating aspects of their sexual interest and behavior into an awareness of themselves. Such people therefore do not engage in behavior on a complete understanding of themselves (sic)"; Craig A. Hill, *Human Sexuality: Personality and Social Psychological Perspectives* (Los Angeles: Sage, 2008), 208.

29 Halperin, *How to Do the History of Homosexuality*, 17.

30 For Halperin, Westerners are unable to think of sexual object-choice beyond a sexual identity that derives, in turn, from fixed sexual orientations; ibid., 98.

31 Sherry Larkins, and Cathy Reback, "Maintaining a Heterosexual Identity: Sexual Meanings Among a Sample of Heterosexually Identified Men Who Have Sex with Men," *Archives of Sexual Behavior* 39, no. 3 (2010): 766–73.

32 Reback and Larkins conclude that here heterosexual identity remains uncompromised by way of compartmentalizing the sexual encounters and keeping them outside the realm of intimacy (Ibid., 771).

33 In contradistinction to Halperin: "Homosexuality is now set over against heterosexuality. Homosexual object-choice, in and of itself, is seen as marking a difference from heterosexual object-choice. Homo- and heterosexuality have become more or less mutually exclusive forms of human subjectivity, different kinds of human sexuality, and any feeling of expression of heterosexual desire is thought to rule out any feeling or expression of homosexual desire on the part of the individual, with the exception of 'bisexuals' (who are therefore thought of as belonging to an entirely separate 'sexuality' [. . .] Homosexuality is part of a new system of sexuality, which functions as a means of personal individuation: it assigns to each individual a sexual orientation and a sexual identity"; Halperin, *How to Do the History of Homosexuality*, 134.

34 In reflecting on historiography from this perspective, Valerie Traub notes that "the incoherences of erotic identities generally are papered over in an attempt to uphold binary gender as the privileged indicator of emotional affect and erotic desire. Despite the common-sense appeal of finding in the biological sex of one's erotic partner the prime indicator of 'sexual orientation,' desire, I believe, is not easily oriented. Both desire and its related gender identifications can transit across identity categories and, following indeterminate trajectories, produce configurations of eroticisms eccentric to the binaries of sex (male/female), gender (masculine/feminine), and sexuality (hetero/homo)"; Valerie Traub, *The Renaissance of Lesbianism in Early Modern England*, Cambridge Studies in Renaissance Literature and Culture (Cambridge; New York: Cambridge University Press, 2002), 14. Similarly, Dinshaw proposes a vision of history where present and past identities juxtapose and touch upon each other because what we consider under the rubric of "sex" is always dependent on cultural phenomena and thus contradictory and fractured. Carolyn Dinshaw, *Getting Medieval:*

Sexualities and Communities, Pre- and Postmodern (Durham, NC: Duke University Press, 1999), 12.

35 Halperin, *How to Do the History of Homosexuality*, 140. Emphasis mine.

36 Ibid., 196.

37 Notice here how Halperin supports his argument by posing past and present as mutually exclusive systems: "The paederast's capacity to eroticize elements of the human anatomy independently of the sex of the person whose anatomy is being eroticized," And later he adds that "we" are unable to relate to such configurations because "most bourgeois Westerners nowadays tend to think of sexual object-choice as an expression of individual 'sexuality,' a fixed sexual disposition or orientation, over which no one has much (if any) control and for which reasons cannot be given: any reasons one might give for one's sexual object-choice seem to be mere afterthoughts, adventitious rationalizations, late cognitive arrivals on the scene of sexual speciation (. . .) Thus, sexual preference is not something that one can be argued logically out of or into – least of all by considerations of utility or convenience. And yet, those are precisely the sorts of considerations that Charicles invokes in order to demonstrate that women are superior vehicles of male sexual pleasure," ibid., 98.

38 Eve Kosofsky Sedgwick, "Gender Criticism: What Isn't Gender?" *The Homepage of Eve Kosofsky Sedgwick at Duke University*. 2 February 2012, www. duke.edu/~sedgwic/WRITING/gender.htm.

39 I have taken very seriously Sedgwick's argument that to define someone's sexuality at her expense is "a terribly consequential seizure." Such a move is an integral aspect of the history of homophobia and must be countered by paying close attention to self-reports in order to foster pluralism "on the heavily contested maps of sexual definition"; Sedgwick, "Gender Criticism: What Isn't Gender?" 26.

40 For the same reasons that Halperin has explained so well *versus* Amy Richlin; Halperin, *How to Do the History of Homosexuality*, 156.67.

41 See Carla Freccero, *Queer/Early/Modern* (Durham, NC: Duke University Press, 2006). "Queer Times," in *After Sex? On Writing Since Queer Theory*, eds. Janet E. Halley and Andrew Parker (Durham, NC: Duke University Press, 2011), 17–26.

42 Donna Haraway, "The Persistence of Vision," in *The Visual Culture Reader*, ed. Nicholas Mirzoeff (London; New York: Routledge, 1998), 681. For this use of the "self" in historiography, see Dinshaw, 14. Menon expresses this point masterfully when she asserts that "homosociality" "argues for the haphazard time of desire, resistant to the kind of identitarian legibility that historicism seeks to create for it"; Menon, *Unhistorical Shakespeare*, 3.

43 Fradenburg and Freccero, *Premodern Sexualities*, xvii. Dinshaw suggests that instead of conceiving historical periods as the beads of a rosary, we would be better served by reverting to Benjamin's image of the "constellation" as a metaphor illustrating the ways in which past events relate to each other and to the present as "starry lights" shining at different times and in different places even as they are perceived at once; Dinshaw, 18. The work of the historian then, she adds, consists of "making pleasurable connections in a context of postmodern indeterminacy," ibid., 36.

44 See here Althaus-Reid. Marcella Althaus-Reid, and Lisa Isherwood, "Thinking Theology and Queer Theory," *Feminist Theology* 15, no. 3 (2007): 302–14.

45 See Chapter 1 for a general assessment of Yarbro Collins's main positions.

46 Yarbro Collins, *Crisis and Catharsis: The Power of the Apocalypse*.

47 John G. Gager, *Kingdom and Community: The Social World of Early Christianity* (Englewood Cliffs: Prentice-Hall, 1975), 51.

48 Pippin explains that the desire of the male who views the Whore's erotic power is restrained by the angel in 17:7. Tina Pippin, *Death and Desire: The Rhetoric of Gender in the Apocalypse of John*, 1st ed. (Louisville: Westminster/John Knox Press, 1992), 22.

49 Ibid., 57.

50 Ibid., 67.

51 "God and the Lamb, the 144,000 males, the good female images, and the evil female images along with those males who are seduced by them. The desire of the true believer is to enter the heavenly city (the Bride). But there is erotic tension at this point; there is distancing from the female; entrance into the female is future and is possible only if the group of men who desire her remain sexually pure and undefiled by women," ibid., 72.

52 Ibid., 73.

53 Ibid. She further adds that the text conveys an ideology of desire that fosters the destruction of the empire along with the destruction of the sexual power of the female.

54 Schüssler Fiorenza, *Sharing Her Word: Feminist Biblical Interpretation in Context* (Boston: Beacon Press, 1998), 37–40.

55 Pippin, *Death and Desire: The Rhetoric of Gender in the Apocalypse of John*, 83.

56 Stephen D. Moore, "Metonymies of Empire: Sexual Humiliation and Gender Masquerade in the Book of Revelation," in *Postcolonial Interventions: Essays in Honor of R. S. Sugirtharajah* (Sheffield, UK: Sheffield Phoenix Press, 2009), 77.

57 Ibid., 86.

58 Ibid., 87.

59 Ibid., 89.

60 "One must avoid absolutizing and universalizing gender as a basic category of analysis," Elisabeth Schüssler Fiorenza, *The Book of Revelation: Justice and Judgment*, 2nd ed. (Minneapolis, MN: Fortress Press, 1998), 215–16.

61 Ibid., 217.

62 Ibid., 221.

63 Ibid., 222.

64 Ibid., 218.

65 Ibid., 210; *Rhetoric and Ethic: The Politics of Biblical Studies*, 19; *Jesus and the Politics of Interpretation* (New York: Continuum, 2000), 23.

66 *The Power of the Word: Scripture and the Rhetoric of Empire* (Minneapolis, MN: Fortress Press, 2007), 252.

67 This critique has been leveled by Fowl; Stephen E. Fowl, "The Ethics of Interpretation, or What's Left Over After the Elimination of Meaning," in *Bible in Three Dimensions: Essays in Celebration of Forty Years of Biblical Studies in the University of Sheffield* (Sheffield, UK: Sheffield University Press, 1990), 379–98.

68 My approach is, once again, Foucauldian. For a critique of Schüssler Fiorenza from this perspective, see David A. Kaden, "Foucault, Feminism, and Liberationist Religion: Discourse, Power, and the Politics of Interpretation in the Feminist Emancipatory Project of Elisabeth Schüssler Fiorenza," *Neotestamentica* 46, no. 1 (2012): 100–03.

69 Schüssler Fiorenza, *The Power of the Word: Scripture and the Rhetoric of Empire*, 59.

70 Erin Runions, *The Babylon Complex: Theopolitical Fantasies of War, Sex, and Sovereignty*, 1st ed. (New York: Fordham University Press, 2014).

71 She mentions the following: (a) The tower of Babel as the human achievement disrupted by God resulting in linguistic diversity. (b) The Empire of Nebuchadnezzar II and the allure of its capital. The Babylonian Empire with its conquest

of Israel, the destroying of the temple, and the taking of the people into Exile shaped the prophetic literature. (3) "The alluring, genderqueer, bloodfiend Whore of Babylon as an allegory for Rome" (4) The mostly nonbiblical, charismatic, yet frightening non/human Antichrist who is said to reside in Babylon; ibid., 2.

72 Ibid., 180.
73 Jasbir K. Puar, *Terrorist Assemblages: Homonationalism in Queer Times*, Next Wave (Durham, NC: Duke University Press, 2007).
74 Junaid Akram Rana, *Terrifying Muslims: Race and Labor in the South Asian Diaspora* (Durham, NC: Duke University Press, 2011).
75 Runions, *The Babylon Complex: Theopolitical Fantasies of War, Sex, and Sovereignty*, 202.
76 Ibid., 206.
77 Ibid., 212.
78 Ibid., 44.
79 "A different mode of reading the Babel/Babylon symbol and its queer cast of associated characters (the antichrist and the Whore), one that keeps at its center the ungovernable, queer, sublime impossibility of knowing truth, or evil," ibid., 214.
80 A Babelian approach to scripture takes uncertainty about transcendental truths as the starting point; ibid., 215.
81 Ibid., 227.
82 Ibid., 236.
83 Ibid., 9.
84 Lee Edelman, *No Future: Queer Theory and the Death Drive* (Durham, NC: Duke University Press, 2004).
85 Leo Bersani, *Is the Rectum a Grave? And Other Essays* (Chicago; London: The University of Chicago Press, 2010).
86 Runions, *The Babylon Complex: Theopolitical Fantasies of War, Sex, and Sovereignty*, 242.
87 Ibid., 243.
88 Ibid., 19.
89 Ibid., 37.
90 Ibid., 236.
91 Flesh and blood readers, to put in the words of Fernando Segovia. See Fernando F. Segovia, "Toward a Hermeneutics of the Diaspora: A Hermeneutics of Otherness and Engagement," in *Reading from This Place (Vol. 1): Social Location and Biblical Interpretation in the United States*, eds. Fernando F. Segovia and Mary Ann Tolbert (Minneapolis, MN: Fortress, 1995), 57–74. The most remarkable contribution to a queer contextual approach to Rev 17–18 is Huber, "Gazing at the Whore: Reading Revelation Queerly," in *Bible Trouble: Queer Reading at the Boundaries of Biblical Scholarship*, eds. Ken Stone and Teresa J. Hornsby (Atlanta: Society of Biblical Literature, 2011). Huber's argument offers a fitting balance to my somewhat male-centered approach to queer criticism.
92 Schüssler Fiorenza, *Rhetoric and Ethic: The Politics of Biblical Studies*, 28.
93 Ibid.
94 Segovia, "Toward a Hermeneutics of the Diaspora," 58.
95 G. K. Beale, *Revelation: A Commentary on the Greek Text*, The New International Greek Testament Commentary (Grand Rapids: W.B. Eerdmans, 1998), 848–49.
96 Besides the examples explored in Chapter 3, it is worth mentioning that John draws heavily upon prophetic literature. For instance, Isa 23:17 describes Tyre as playing the harlot with the kingdoms of the earth, conflating, once again,

the economic, political, religious, and sexual dimensions: "fornicate" seems to refer to "intercourse with other nations". Similar resonances are found in Ezek 16:1–36 and 27:27.

97 Leon Morris, *Revelation: An Introduction and Commentary* (Downers Grove: IVP Academic, 2007), 205.
98 Beale, *Revelation*, 852, n. 17. As Beale argues: "He had to paint these characters of evil in such horrid form so that the saints would not be too easily attracted,".
99 Mounce, *The Book of Revelation*, 307.
100 Beale, *Revelation*, 862–63.
101 See also 12:12; 22: 6–7, 12.
102 Christopher A. Frilingos, *Spectacles of Empire: Monsters, Martyrs, and the Book of Revelation*, Divinations (Philadelphia: University of Pennsylvania Press, 2004), 50–2.
103 It is worth noticing that in Revelation 17 authority (ἐξουσία) is attributed to the kings (17:12) and they will give it to the Beast (17:13). Also the angel "cried out in a strong voice" highlighting the contrast between the authority coming from heaven and the demise of the earthly kingdom.
104 Beale, *Revelation*, 884–87.
105 Ibid., 895.
106 Ibid., 906.
107 Craig A. Williams, *Roman Homosexuality: Ideologies of Masculinity in Classical Antiquity* (New York: Oxford University Press, 1998).
108 See, for instance, how 19:20 mentions that those who were "deceived" by the Beast "are thrown alive into the lake of fire."

5 Conclusion

Manifesting Revelation among the manifestos

Manifesting time: introducing contemporary manifestos on biblical studies

My argument throughout has assumed that the biblical text is a relevant, powerful, widely propagated ideological tool. In material terms, the Bible is the object of a multibillion industry devoted to the dissemination of the biblical texts for all kinds of ideological, political, economic, and cultural purposes. I refer to this reality as the "biblical industrial complex" as a way of embracing the variety of institutions and practices that are supported by trillions of dollars of investments in both propagating and eliminating the biblical text and its influences. The enterprise of dispersing the biblical text at all different levels (cultural, economic, political, sociological) takes place worldwide and without interruption.[1]

The BSIC (Biblical Studies Industrial Complex) encompasses all faith-based endeavors and academic approaches, orality as much as writing, the objective as much as the subjective, the public as much as the private. Daily, thousands of books are published, sermons are preached, biblical arguments of all sorts are made, courses designed, professors hired, conferences, seminars, and lectures presented. In some cases, even governments base their arguments on various versions and interpretations of the biblical messages. In sum, the cultural influence of this one book manifests itself globally in the shaping of our cultural worldview, funded by a multibillion industrial complex. This dimension of biblical interpretation is important to my argument because, for practical purposes, it demonstrates that the Bible is in itself an exceptional text and should, as such, be deployed to the advancement of progressive politics.

Biblical scholarship has not been particularly diligent about scrutinizing its own conditions of possibility. One way in which the biblical industrial complex represses reflection on its conditions of possibility is through the idea of "objectivity." The retrieval of the original meaning of the text (regardless of the theory of meaning behind the enterprise), or even its potential impact across time and space (reception history), has paid no attention to the fact that the only reason such scholarship is possible is because the Bible is not a book with an objective meaning, but a book with a cultural and religious history. To put it differently, the Bible is widely studied in objective/historical terms only because the Bible is crucial in subjective/cultural contexts. The current study of the Bible as a text of the past is possible only because of the construction of the biblical text in the present.[2]

Biblical studies: the question of the present

The development of biblical studies in the last quarter of the twentieth century has ended the monopoly of the historical-critical approach. The eruption of contextual and ideological criticism in the 1980s and '90s not only questioned the objectivistic agenda of historical, sociological, and literary methods but also introduced contemporary concerns into the study of the Bible. The impact of "theory" in biblical studies has also contributed to the implementation of historiographical models that have bridged the gap between the present and the past. Recently, it seems, the convoluted methodological and theoretical map of biblical studies has triggered the publication of different "manifestos" that, in one way or another, tackle the contradictions produced by such a state of affairs. One could possibly argue that the late appearance of such manifestos evinces disorientation in the field, a lack of clear direction, a crisis in imagination.[3] In what follows, I introduce, chronologically, four different attempts to take stock of biblical studies as a discipline and corresponding proposals regarding where the field should head. After the presentation of each manifesto, I will underline their respective stances on the relevance of the present in the interpretation of the past. My ultimate goal is to situate, compare, and evaluate these different positions in relationship to the arguments made about Revelation.

Dale Martin: biblical studies within a theological scope

Dale Martin's *Pedagogy of the Bible* is grounded in an empirical survey of the various hermeneutical approaches that professors in different theological institutions employ when researching, teaching, and writing about the Bible. Martin conducted his research in ten different schools, thus offering a snapshot of the real state of "biblical education." Martin finds that "historical criticism" is still the dominant methodological approach to Scripture, although professors and students alike occasionally look in different directions when it comes to applying the exegetical findings. Historical criticism, he notes, considers the primary meaning of the text to be what would have been understood by the original ancient audience, what the author intended.[4] Martin also names some of the fears that historical criticism seeks to shrug off – mainly anachronism and eisegesis – for the sake of looking at the texts anew, freeing them from self-serving and overly familiar interpretations.[5]

Furthermore, Martin identifies as the main gap in biblical interpretation the lack of theoretical training, the great failure in theological education.[6]

The lack of training in the theory of biblical interpretation leads to professors and students at the surveyed institutions to believe that the historical method is the only way of making meaning out of the texts. The result of considering historical criticism as the main/only approach to the texts, Martin argues, is twofold: a serious lack of ability to engage the Bible in theologically creative ways and a compartmentalization of the field of biblical studies, both of which end up isolating the discipline, not only in terms of its relationship to other theological disciplines but also in relationship to the community of believers.

Martin looks to premodern times for inspiration. He surveys some important premodern theological thinkers to propose ways to approach the text that loosen the grasp of the historical monopoly on the current state of the discipline.[7] Martin highlights what we can learn in the present from the forefathers of creative exegesis is new ways to relate to scripture (not as an object, but as space to live in, or pray with, etc.) in order to expand "Christian imagination."

Martin's solution to what he sees as the main problem (the historical criticism monopoly) includes several measures that are to be implemented in the theological curriculum. These measures include: an integration of the historical approach with (and among) other methods, an incorporation of different disciplines (history, literature, art, etc.) and their contemporary methodological assumptions, instruction on the theology of scripture before the methodology of interpretation, and the introduction of theoretical frames of literary theory. Finally, Martin advocates an integration of scripture within other creative disciplines such as art, literature, and music.[8]

One way in which Martin suggests integrating the biblical texts with broader theological/Christian themes is by exercising certain hermeneutical approaches of a theological nature. It is not my goal to offer here a description of the rules that Martin explores;[9] suffice it to say that, with regard to the role of Scripture in the present and its potential for resistance, Martin strongly advocates relevance exclusively within the Christian community. Theology he defines in the narrow sense of religious beliefs/experiences that link the community with God. There is no trace of the political/ethical impact of the Bible as a whole for the present outside the church or its institutional setting (whether Protestant or Catholic).

Roland Boer: biblical studies within a political scope

Boer, the most salient theorist of Marxism and biblical interpretation,[10] starts his manifesto with a bold claim that picks up right where Dale Martin left off: biblical studies have been institutionally colonized by church and theology.[11] His diagnosis of biblical studies as a field takes as its point of departure an evaluation that, with some nuances, contradicts Martin's evaluation and solution: everyone assumes that biblical studies is based on a religious commitment, that biblical studies continues to be a part of theology, and that such a situation is supported in institutions with theological programs.

Boer then starts his reflection guided by the following heuristic question: "What would biblical studies look like if it was not tied to religious commitment, theology, or theological institutions."[12] Whereas Martin calls for an insertion of biblical studies into theology as a solution to the problems in the discipline, Boer bluntly calls for an emancipation of biblical studies from the theological arena. The colonization of theology has impeded a radical development of the discipline that, in turn, needs to be scrutinized through a hermeneutics of suspicion applied at every level of interpretation: "the ideological force of the texts must be accounted for, criticized and where necessary resisted as part of the process of interpretation itself."[13]

Boer proposes a solution for adoption in the institutional/disciplinary framework: a complete interaction of the discipline with literary, cultural, philosophical, legal, historical, and social scientific studies. Such development should be expanded beyond the institutional to the level of the masses, taking the Bible back to the people in the tradition of liberationist hermeneutics. The movement of dissociating biblical studies from theology and returning it to "the world" leads, in Boer's mind, to new possibilities: the Bible understood as a place where the religious left can establish alliance with progressive movements that are engaged in the ideological/political battles of equal distribution, hunger, poverty, and exploitation of all kinds. In Boer's view, the readings of the Bible by the secular and the religious left would affirm the tradition of revolutionary inspiration that comes from the Bible."[14]

On the ideological/theological level, Boer stands in clear opposition to Martin's proposal. Whereas the later calls for an integration of biblical studies within the church and theology, Boer calls for disintegration. Whereas for Martin historical criticism is the problem, for Boer the problem lies not so much in methodology but in the larger playing field. Whereas Martin does not theorize the political impact of the Bible, for Boer this is the question of biblical studies itself. There is an impetus in Martin's argument towards the center, whereas for Boer the direction of the Bible is outwards, towards the margins.

Stephen Moore and Yvonne Sherwood: biblical studies within a theoretical scope

Stephen D. Moore and Yvonne Sherwood are both tested representatives of post-structuralist, theory-laden approaches to biblical studies. Accordingly, *The Invention of the Biblical Scholar*[15] is a suitable corollary to their groundbreaking contributions to the field, inasmuch as they, in autocritical fashion, question some of their own long-held assumptions and advance a new direction for the field that might stand at odds with some of their respective previous proposals. Once again, it is not my intention to explore in detail their many insightful arguments but rather to locate their work broadly within the range of manifestos in order to understand their articulation of the present.

Moore and Sherwood sketch a genealogical history – Foucauldian style – of the field of biblical studies. They start with a straightforward diagnosis of the field by stating that the use of theory in biblical studies, despite its advancements, has never quite made it into the field.[16] The deployment of theory in biblical studies is the uniting factor in the analysis of the different methodological approaches that have subsequently been adopted within the discipline. The authors pay special attention to the evolution of the historical-critical methods and recent developments of literary theory in biblical studies, focusing on what it is specific to the field itself.

One of their arguments is that the proliferation of "methodolatry" has had the effect (intended, they argue) of separating the biblical scholar from laity, while keeping disciplinary boundaries unchallenged. To put it differently, the deployment of theory in biblical studies has perpetuated deeply ingrained trends within the discipline such as provincialism and elitism. Theory has kept the churchly masses at bay.[17] The imperative "to be fruitful and multiply methodologically"[18] has particularly affected contextual approaches and clouded their political impact. In effect, the result has been that the proliferation of "readings from this place" has reinforced the traditional core of the discipline and has provincialized the readings. As they argue, although contextualism is centrally concerned with social justice, its situatedness goes against the notion of universal justice and human rights.[19]

The chapter that remains to be written, the authors argue, is one in which the Bible is situated at the center of the philosophical enterprise, a task that is being carried out by outsiders who have concerned themselves with situating the Bible at the center of the theory. "The return to the Bible" in philosophy is revolutionary because it situates at the center what has been traditionally excluded.[20] The pursuit of such scholarly enterprise would be the perfect antidote to the "Enlightenment Bible," which the authors, following Sheehan, understand to be the Bible viewed as a cultural authority.[21]

Moore and Sherwood's genealogical analysis is, in my view, very helpful in terms of mapping the current state of affairs in biblical studies. Their solution to the problems detected, however, falls short and ends up being very disappointing, if not contradictory to their own assumptions. Whereas they affirm that the role of theory in biblical studies has been to provide a patina of authority to biblical scholars, so that interpretation was not confused with preaching and the professional was not conflated with the lay, their final and unique proposal for philosophical ethics to cure "the shamanism" in biblical studies is likely to perpetuate biblical studies' isolation and keep at bay those trends within biblical studies that might contribute to the advancement of a discipline concerned with contemporary issues.

Fernando Segovia: biblical studies within a global scope

The question of the present is at the center of Fernando Segovia's latest contribution to biblical studies – the role of biblical criticism in critical times. "The present" is conceptualized as a time of crisis, given the dramatic and one could say apocalyptic, historic events of the twentieth century. The sequence of the world wars and the global migratory movements from the Global South towards the North exemplify the plight of contemporaneity and, as such, the critical moments that demand a response on behalf of the critic.[22]

The relationship between the task of biblical criticism and "worldly" events is introduced by summarizing how different presidential addresses have referred to coetaneous events. The indictment is clear: despite their obvious learned skills, "in critical times presidents have kept the world of criticism and the world of politics quite apart from each other."[23] From the perspective of the intellectual, Segovia appropriately takes Said's analysis as a point of departure to establish that the function of the intellectual is one in which she or he "is defined as representing a message to and for a public," privileging the marginalized within structures of power within the global economy.[24] The role of the biblical critic in the present, subsequently, seems to be that of an agent that bridges the gap between the past and the present, a present conceptualized as conflictual. The role of the biblical critic, and more broadly of criticism as a whole, is characterized as activism.

The present is characterized as going through series of crises in all spheres of life. Such global contexts call for a theorization through the lens of the Global South, through the heuristic and hermeneutical tools of critical theories developed by the victims of the globalization process. The work of Alfred López provides a starting point for this theorization of the post-Global South whose reality of impoverishment and material injustice has triggered, among many other things, mass migrations and abysmal wealth gaps. The role of the intellectual is consequently to reflect on the conditions of these groups and to explain their identity and the causes of their plight with the perspective set on the future. The utopian accent should not go unnoticed.[25]

The proposal for biblical studies shall take a global approach as reflected in the epistemologies of the South: beyond the West, beyond hegemonic knowledge, and beyond monological knowledge for "only through such plurality of knowledges, grounded in their historical trajectories and not the universal history of the West, can a vision of utopia arise for the future of the world."[26]

The paradigm, temporarily defined as "global-systemic," is built upon the dialogue between biblical criticism and the global scene, "from and for the unique (. . .) critical times in which we find ourselves."[27] Such an enterprise calls for an expansive interdisciplinary dialogue that incorporates the theorizations of the different crises and the world theories of the North and the South. The goal, as it affects the critic and, by extension, criticism, is to "make a pact of blood with the world."[28]

Segovia addresses and theorizes the question of the present as no other biblical critic does, perhaps with the exception of Roland Boer. To Segovia the topic of the present is not an addendum but a priority that informs his approach, his methodology, and his heuristic and hermeneutical movements. The direction is not so much from past to present but backwards. In other words, the question of the present is not a mere supplement to a theological/ideological reflection but a guiding concern that determines the methodological approach.

Segovia had previously theorized, among other topics, contextual readings in general, with particular attention to Latino readings and postcolonial approaches. Here he steps on to the global scene on the back of a metadiscourse that seeks to integrate these readings of the biblical texts and their discursive and material implications within the globality of the present. One particular insight of his has informed my approach to the biblical text: the starting point, not only chronologically but thematically and ideologically, is the question of the present. The text is not the point of departure but it is a dense point of conflictual interpretations, illuminated from different perspectives and problematics and, as such, a constructed web of meanings with diverse ideological and political consequences for the interpretative community.

Revelation: the question of the present

The issue of the present Empire and Revelation, that is, the scholarly debate over its emancipatory potential that was introduced in Chapter 1, has been the guiding point throughout my presentation. I turn now to contextualize the arguments I proposed in light of scholars' visions for the future of biblical studies regarding its relationship with the present. What are the implications of tackling the question of the emancipatory potential of Revelation?

Recently, Susan Hylen has tackled the issue as it pertains to the violent imagery in Revelation. She takes issue with scholars who argue that the violent imagery of Revelation is subsumed within a pacific language.[29] She says that those scholars who sweep violence under the rug operate with an inadequate model of metaphoricity in that they tend to understand metaphors as standing for something else, regardless of their form. Metaphors, conceptual metaphor theory argues, are not simply decorative but add essential meaning; they "invite the reader into a way of seeing the world."[30] Regarding Revelation, what is dangerous is that violent imagery triggers violent readings/attitudes: conquering, winning over enemies, and so forth, are part of the book's rhetoric no matter how we do away with violence.

Hylen argues that different metaphors highlight different aspects of the book without canceling each other out, and so offer a poliphonous song of different and oppositional evocative meanings. Hylen ultimately argues that this is ethically productive in that violence is canceled, nuanced, and complexified, opening the door to multiple interpretations. Hylen situates this possibility within "context theory," concluding that it is "useful in contexts in which ethical action demands recognition of the moral complexity of the situation."[31] Metaphor theory consequently calls for discernment in contextual terms.

Hylen's final solution to the question of Revelation's implications for the present is consistent with my approach to Revelation throughout the preceding chapters, providing a literary solution to an ethical conundrum: how are we, after all, to interpret the political force of Revelation in current times? Such a position had previously been theorized by Stephen Moore, who in an earlier manifesto to the one presented in the previous section proposed contextual hermeneutics of the cultural studies sort as the destabilizer of the status quo.[32]

In his opinion, literary studies of the queer, masculinist, postcolonial, and cultural studies kind have offered an antidote to the obsession of biblical studies with methodology. Particularly compelling in this older argument is that ideological approaches do not offer a methodology but, together with feminist studies, provide us with "a critical sensibility, an encompassing angle of vision that, in a more fundamental fashion than a methodological framework, brings previously unperceived or disavowed data into focus."[33] The demise of methodology, Moore ventured, would bring down the walls that keep academia and church apart, and that is the challenge that we need to face: the need to write biblical scholarship without method, without falling into preaching. The key, he argues here (although he will later dismiss it) is "contextual hermeneutics," both as a remedy to method and to the focus on the text.[34]

Moore and Hylen are particularly relevant to my project, because, in suggesting "contextual hermeneutics" as the solution, they identify the present as the major concern of Revelation Studies. Moore, arguably one of the most sophisticated thinkers on theory and the Bible, identifies "practice" as the solution to theory. What he fails to see is that the biblical texts are already enmeshed in a network of practical readings, which, as Boer and Segovia have shown, need to be accounted for. Furthermore, "emancipatory hermeneutics" provides a unique opportunity, given its solid trajectory within biblical studies, as a springboard to think further about the role of the Bible in culture. To put it differently, not only do cultural studies outside of biblical scholarship have something to offer; the other way around is also true. Liberationist hermeneutics, I would argue – given its thorough theorization of the relationship between textual meaning, reading strategies, and political and ethical reflection – offers a unique opportunity to theorize the biblical text and, as Hylen points out, is the only possible way to evaluate Revelation's ethical clout. I turn now to recapitulate the arguments I presented on Revelation in light of the insights provided by the theoretical work in the broader field of biblical studies.

Empire and subjectivity

Chapter 2 takes as its point of departure the problematic of Empire, that is, the current theorization of the global economy, especially as it pertains to the inequalities of economic, politic, and social structures. My overall concern here is twofold: on the theoretical side, I am concerned with the ways in which we can think about agency in the context of political problems that surpass any individual practice. On the practical side, alongside the liberationist hermeneutics developed by Boer and Segovia, the chapter explores a way in which readers and interpreters can deploy the biblical texts as sources of resistance, as templates to envision new approaches to pressing cultural and political problems.

My goal in taking up Hardt and Negri's conceptualization of Empire is not to offer a comprehensive, monological, unilateral theorization of demanding contemporary political issues, but to tentatively continue an incipient dialogue between the influence of the biblical text and the current state of affairs. To put it more bluntly: *Empire* provides a comprehensive framework to start theorizing a resistant subjectivity that mines past resisting subjectivities as examples of what a subject in the present might look like. It is in this regard that Foucauldian ethics prove to be crucial in my argument.

Against the backdrop of a controlling society that has blurred the distinction between inside/out and has caused a subjectivity that is always enmeshed in the circuits of control, a society where desire has been construed to serve the interests of global capitalism, contemporary theories of subjectivity call for an "anthropological exodus." Such an exodus seems to be happening de facto in different ways, and it is the role of the critic to account for those existing practices as well as to provide historical, cultural, and political knowledge about the ways in which our past can inform and enhance such practices.

To study the New Testament as a source of subject formation in the present is not new, but it is a project that has not, in my view, reached its full potential. Furthermore, there is specificity about the biblical text that most critics (from the left at least) gloss over and do not take into consideration when doing high criticism: the fact that the biblical text is read, interpreted, deployed, taught, and examined to shape what I have called the "industrial biblical complex." The biblical text is, unlike any other text, a text that is disseminated throughout culture holds an unrivaled political potential.

Foucault's approach is particularly relevant to the project of interpreting the texts from this perspective, because, as much as he opposes any plain emancipatory project, his perspective comprehensively theorizes the turning points between subject formation and subject resistance. At the biblical level, this insight can be interpreted as arguing that the negative/positive influence of the biblical text is the space where the subject can turn it into political resistance/collaboration. One could possibly argue that this is the ideological thrust behind Foucault's philosophical project in general, and the history of sexuality in particular. If the task of the historian is the unearthing of under-histories of unity and purity, I can hardly think of a better text than Revelation to offer a minority report on the situation of the first-century Roman Empire.

Such a project pitches Foucault against himself for, as has been widely argued, he misconstrued and flattened the complex history of first-century Christianity. Halvor Moxnes took up the task of exploring what a Foucauldian approach to Paul for the purposes of subject formation might look like. Beyond the merits and deficiencies of such an approach as explored in Chapter 2, what interests me here is to point out the implications of the approach for emancipatory biblical criticism in general.

Moxnes seems to underline certain values that run against the current of contemporary Euro-American politics. He sees Paul's image of the body as essentially heteronomous, thus counteracting any anthropological claim of the body in individualistic, goal-oriented, monadic terms. Furthermore, Pauline ethics offer the underside of Empire by opposing marital values and offering an alternative to the elitism of Foucault's sources.

I have applied the current ethical concern regarding the oversaturation of subjectivity by Empire to Revelation, throwing into relief the oppositional nature of the technologies of subject formation: the lack of apodictic rules, the disavowal of household mores, asceticism against an economic system that promotes luxury, the nature of the colonized selfhood that finds its resolution through utopia, and an uncompromising sexual ethics that is anti-imperial in nature (regardless of the downside of its outcome).

I have pointed out the risk of interpreting Revelation in Manichean terms – the Whore versus the Lamb. Such an approach is granted by the text itself, especially when the metaphors are posed against each other. The focus on subject formation, however, alleviates oppositional readings (good vs. evil) through its understanding of the demise of the Whore as the demise of ideals of wealth, luxury, and excess.

In sum, the context of the present Empire, the relationship between subject formation and macropolitical entities, and the realization that theory in the present finds an incomparable ethical source in the past guides my ethical-contextual approach. Unlike Martin who restricts the biblical text to the theological community, and Moore who turns to high theory as the savior of biblical hermeneutics, I understand the text as potentially imbedded in grassroots movements of all kinds and venues. Boer's argument that the biblical hermeneutics need to be rescued for the left and Segovia's insight that global issues must be at the center of the hermeneutical task prove to be heuristically rich when interpreting Revelation.

Capitalism and sexual identity

Whereas Chapter 2 explored the cultural and political links between Empire and subject formation, Chapter 3 seeks to tighten up those connections by introducing a framework that facilitates the exploration of bodily resistance and economic systems, whether capitalism in the present or agrarian economies in the past.

Capitalism, theorists have been arguing, has, with its modeling of gender roles in general and its influence on the development of procreative patterns in particular, created sexual identities as such. D'Emilio, for instance, argues that the decoupling of sex from procreation leads to conceptualizing sexuality around playful desire. Such a split, Hennessy argues, has turned into a commodification of sexual identities, giving rise to identities that suit the flows of the market. Furthermore, as Lowe puts it, subject formation is deeply intertwined with the appropriation of sexuality as designed towards desiring capitalistic objects: subject formation, then, is turned into objectification itself.

The figure of the harlot serves as a paradigmatic example of the connections between subject formation and political and economic macrostructures. The harlot is not necessarily an "identity," although it can be, but a point of convergence for sexuality, gender, nationality, class, etc. In the Hebrew Bible, the foreign harlot symbolizes a threat that endangers national and religious boundaries. There is no better example of this than the figure of Gomer in Hosea. Notwithstanding the multiple interpretations of Gomer, the harlot is a trope of a religious/national identity, and her domestication a metaphor of what the collective group should do. The evaluation of such a rich metaphor in ethical terms is riddled with complexities, because, if it is true, as Gail Yee argues, that Hosea identifies the whore with the elite (thus enacting a ferocious critique of the elite powers), the use of the trope reinforces the image of womanhood as plagued with inordinate desire.

Jezebel and Rahab, as foreign women in exercise of power, are portrayed under some of the same circumstances. Whereas Jezebel embodies nationalistic anxieties against foreign powers, Rahab incarnates the desire to construct a national identity on the reality of the conquest. In any case, the harlot is also an effective metaphor, because her surplus of desire brings the author and the reader into a dialogue about the effects of her actions. In effect, the need to contain the excesses of desire initiated by the author is replicated in the reader's adherence to a textual ideology that criticizes religious and economic idolatry, commercial trade, miscegenation, or pernicious political structures.

The polyvalent meaning of the whore in the Hebrew Bible is brought to bear on the analysis of the Whore of Babylon. Revelation is consistent in its portrayal of the whore as a trope for imperial economy with the goal of shaping the audience dis/identifications with Babylon/the Lamb. Continuing the observations of subject formation made in Chapter 2, I am particularly interested in the third chapter to point at the ways in which Revelation is ultimately an invitation to steer desire away from Empire, while forging ways of experimenting with desire that build on the stigmatization of the low-ranked sexual worker or on the disidentification with the Empress who sits on a throne.

The question of the configuration of desire is particularly relevant to the issue of subject formation in the context of capitalist culture. I have been arguing that Revelation should be used in the ethical project of thinking of new ways of subject formation. Consequently, Revelation 17–18 offer a particularly suitable example of how an ancient text aims at shaping its audience's desire, but also how it can be deployed as a critical tool to think about how contemporary readers position themselves vis-à-vis the strategic rhetorical moves of Revelation in terms of its disidentification with any character who mourns the demise of the Whore.

Revelation proves to be helpful in this regard because it reshapes sexual desire/economic desire through affective drives. Unlike in contemporary Western capitalist societies where desire, as Hennessy puts it, is at the service of wealth growth, Revelation offers an example of sexual desire geared towards a critique of wealth itself. To put it differently, Revelation can be interpreted as an invitation to reconceptualize desire as a monological enterprise exclusively concerned with pleasure.

The problem is once again philosophical in nature with important political ramifications. In relationship to the manifestos explored, again the scope of the question tackled surpasses the narrow constraints of Martin's conceptualization of biblical studies within the theological realm and Moore and Sherwood's circumscription of biblical hermeneutics to the realm of theory. Explicitly aligned with Boer's proposal of biblical studies as offering ways in which the text can be deployed to counteract regressive politics and Segovia's project of situating the task of the critic at the core of our world's crisis, I argue that the figure of the harlot serves as a fulcrum to conceptualize sex at the intersection of Empire and subjectivity.

Desire's mobility

The question of the present, as most contemporary biblical scholars put it, demands a proper contextualization. Whereas for Schüssler Fiorenza the present is theorized around the rhetorical effects of the text within the context of kyriarchy, for Martin the present demands reading scripture in broader theological terms. Boer, for his part, seeks a Marxist reading of the present that is propelled by a liberationist approach to Scripture, while for Segovia, one could argue, the present is the only concern.

Critics of contextual hermeneutics fault this approach for being subjective, localist, and for fostering eisegesis rather than exegesis. They claim that, although it is impossible to leave behind the Weltanschauung of the interpreter, it is the role of theoretical hermeneutics to bracket present concerns in order to achieve an objective understanding of the text. Moore himself has accused contextual ethics of localism and of being politically ineffective because of its circumscription to narrow agendas. Although I agree that contextual ethics need to move beyond the impasse posed by constricted interests, I also argue that marginal experiences may and should be a trigger to theorize the present; that is, they should be used as a fulcrum to undo current hegemonic approaches to theory. Such was my goal in Chapter 4, where, based on specific sexual practices, I attempted to develop a theory of desire that, in turn, allows for a bridging of the gap between the biblical past and contemporary sexual ethics.

Queer theory has explored the appropriation of the past since its inception, and has not only questioned the continuity of "sexuality" as a cultural reality throughout time and space but, more importantly, advanced historiographical models that reflect on the ways in which the present colonizes the past and vice versa. The pressing issue that I address in Chapter 4 is the dislocation of sexual desire at every level outside sexual identities so those who benefit from the privilege of invisibility come to the fore. By offering a comprehensive theoretical framework in which different contexts can be explained, I show how the reader might position herself regarding the sexual ideology and gender configurations of the text. The undecidability of gender and desire results ultimately in the undecidability of interpretation.

Revelation as source of subject formation in empire

If this is the case – if meaning is affixed to gender and desire – what are the consequences of teasing out Revelation as a source of subject formation in the context of Empire? On the one hand, the interpreter is situated within her identity against the text, deciding which paths of desire she is more likely to take; on the other hand, given the multiplicity of identifications, the excess that is disavowed need not be sexual in nature, but could be economic. Only in this way does Revelation acts as a text with politically subversive potential that does not need to replicate hegemonic sexual mores. To rephrase, the decoupling of desire from sexual identity allows for a disavowal of imperial economy while identifying with the queer aspects of the desire routinely expressed in the text.

In terms of the manifestos presented, such a position on Revelation evinces once again that the biblical text needs, on the one hand, to be situated outside the institutional theological boundaries it has been put in, and, on the other, cannot be uniquely explored through the lens of high theory that recoils from the experience of flesh and blood readers. The progressive biblical interpretation advanced by Boer proves to be an appropriate template to think of Revelation as an instance in which sexual ethics can be an ally to the left. The undecidability of desire – that is, the framework where desire does not have unidirectional orientations – opens up a space to consider configurations of desire that transcend the tight boundaries within which the West has operated up to this point. Here the "global-systemic" approach of Segovia is particularly relevant because unhistoricism, if not offering a comprehensive theory of desire, at least undoes the frameworks within which the West has monopolized the question of sexual identity.

The problematic of the present as explored in the manifestos frames the question that was presented in Chapter 1. This opens up the possibility and urgency of evaluating Revelation as a political manifesto of the past with significant ethical consequences for the present, repressed as such concerns may be in most contributions. After outlining broader contexts in the present, Revelation can now be interpreted within the matrix provided, a move that, in turn, brings new light to the hermeneutical conundrums around Rev 17–18: dismissing Revelation as anti-Christian or politically ineffective, as playing into the hands of Empire, or as a hindrance to an ethics of global resistance. These positions ring true only if the global context of the reading/readers provided is opposite to the one I have outlined throughout the different chapters. "Reading contexts" implies "reading contests." Since the indeterminacy of interpretation is grounded in a queer conceptualization of identity (a subject positionality that shifts in time and space) the "Revelation against Empire" I have proposed is subject to reevaluation in changing and different contexts.

Notes

1 This is the other side of the coin of what Hector Avalos calls "bibliolatry." Although he is right to point out that, at the academic level, the Bible is relevant only because of biblical scholars' interests in promoting, he neglects the incommensurable cultural impact of the biblical imaginary. See Hector Avalos, *The End of Biblical Studies* (Amherst: Prometheus Books, 2007).

2 Similarly, as I show in the following sections, the study of the past of biblical studies as a discipline is a present re-construction that, in turn, as Segovia and Boer remind us, is not agreed-upon; Roland Boer, and Fernando F. Segovia, *The Future of the Biblical Past: Envisioning Biblical Studies on a Global Key* (Atlanta, GA: Society of Biblical Literature, 2012), xvi.

3 These manifestos are, in a way, the tip of the iceberg in that they represent, condense, and summarize a body of literature concerned with envisioning a future for the discipled based on an specific mapping of its past; among the most influential: Robert M. Fowler, Edith Waldvogel Blumhofer, and Fernando F. Segovia, *New Paradigms for Bible Study: The Bible in the Third Millennium* (New York: T & T Clark International, 2004); George Aichele, and Bible and Culture Collective, *The Postmodern Bible* (New Haven: Yale University Press, 1995). Elisabeth Schüssler Fiorenza, *Democratizing Biblical Studies: Toward an Emancipatory Educational Space*, 1st ed. (Louisville: Westminster John Knox Press, 2009); John J. Collins, *The Bible After Babel: Historical Criticism in a Postmodern Age* (Grand Rapids, MI: W.B. Eerdmans 2005).

4 Dale B. Martin, *Pedagogy of the Bible: An Analysis and Proposal*, 1st ed. (Louisville: Westminster John Knox Press, 2008), 3–5.

5 Ibid., 14.

6 Ibid., 17.

7 Ibid., 47–69.

8 Similarly to the contributions in Eric D. Barreto, *Reading Theologically: Foundations for Learning*, Foundations for Learning (Minneapolis, MN: Fortress Press, 2014).

9 He mines other authors in order to give some examples of what interpreting the Bible in new ways might look like; Martin, *Pedagogy of the Bible: An Analysis and Proposal*, 81–7.

10 Most notably Roland Boer, *Knockin' on Heaven's Door: The Bible and Popular Culture* (London; New York: Routledge, 1999); *Last Stop Before Antarctica: The Bible and Postcolonialism in Australia* (Sheffield, UK: Sheffield Academic Press, 2001); *Marxist Criticism of the Bible* (London; New York: T&T Clark International, 2003); *Rescuing the Bible*, Blackwell Manifestos (Malden; Oxford: Wiley-Blackwell, 2007); *Criticism of Heaven: On Marxism and Theology* (Leiden; Boston: Brill, 2007).

11 Roland Boer, *Secularism and Biblical Studies* (London; Oakville: Equinox Pub., 2010), 27.

12 Ibid., 29.

13 Ibid., 30.

14 Ibid., 37.

15 Stephen D. Moore, and Yvonne Sherwood, *The Invention of the Biblical Scholar: A Critical Manifesto* (Minneapolis, MN: Fortress Press, 2011).

16 Ibid., 10.

17 This is actually the same claim that James Barr makes regarding the role of historical critical-criticism; See James Barr, *The Concept of Biblical Theology: An Old Testament Perspective* (Minneapolis, MN: Fortress Press, 1999), 401–38.

18 Moore and Sherwood, *The Invention of the Biblical Scholar*, 91.

19 Ibid., 121.

20 The authors are thinking of the works of such scholars as Badiou, Caputo, Blanton, and Agamben.

21 Moore and Sherwood, *The Invention of the Biblical Scholar*, 48.

22 Fernando F. Segovia, "Criticism in Critical Times: Reflections on Vision and Task," *Journal of Biblical Literature* 134, no. 1 (2015): 9.

23 Ibid., 13.

24 Ibid., 15.

25 Ibid., 20.

26 Ibid., 24.

27 Ibid., 29.

28 Ibid.

29 Susan Hylen, "Metaphor Matters: Violence and Ethics in Revelation," *The Catholic Biblical Quarterly* 73, no. 4 (2011): 780.

30 Ibid., 783.

31 Ibid., 793. There are other functions such as the difficulty of conveying theological realities, or underlining the contradictory nature of the divine.

32 Stephen D. Moore, "A Modest Manifesto for New Testament Literary Criticism: How to Interface with a Literary Studies Field That Is Post-Literary, Post-Theoretical, and Post-Methodological," *Biblical Interpretation* 15, no. 1 (2007): 1–25.

33 Ibid., 23.

34 Ibid., 25.

Bibliography

Abernethy, David B., *The Dynamics of Global Dominance: European Overseas Empires, 1415–1980* (New Haven: Yale University Press, 2000).

Aichele, George, Bible, and Culture Collective, *The Postmodern Bible* (New Haven: Yale University Press, 1995).

Althaus-Reid, Marcella, *The Queer God* (London; New York: Routledge, 2003).

Althaus-Reid, Marcella, and Lisa Isherwood, "Thinking Theology and Queer Theory," *Feminist Theology* 15, no. 3 (2007): 302–14.

Andersen, Francis I., and David Noel Freedman, *Hosea, a New Translation with Introduction and Commentary*, 1st ed. (New York: Doubleday, 1980).

Aschkenasy, Nehama, *Woman at the Window: Biblical Tales of Oppression and Escape* (Detroit: Wayne State University Press, 1998).

Aune, David Edward, *Revelation* (Dallas: Word Books, 1997).

———, *Revelation 17–22* (Nashville: T. Nelson, 1998).

Avalos, Hector, *The End of Biblical Studies* (Amherst: Prometheus Books, 2007).

Barclay, William, *The Revelation of John (Vol. 2)* (Louisville: Westminster John Knox Press, 2004).

Barr, James, *The Concept of Biblical Theology: An Old Testament Perspective* (Minneapolis, MN: Fortress Press, 1999).

Barreto, Eric D., *Reading Theologically: Foundations for Learning*, Foundations for Learning (Minneapolis, MN: Fortress Press, 2014).

Bauckham, Richard, *The Climax of Prophecy: Studies on the Book of Revelation* (Edinburgh: T&T Clark, 1993).

———, *The Theology of the Book of Revelation* (Cambridge; New York: Cambridge University Press, 1993).

Beale, G. K., *Revelation: A Commentary on the Greek Text*, The New International Greek Testament Commentary (Grand Rapids, MI: W.B. Eerdmans, 1998).

Benson, Bruce Ellis, and Peter Goodwin Heltzel, eds., *Evangelicals and Empire: Christian Alternatives to the Political Status Quo* (Grand Rapids, MI: Brazos Press, 2008).

Bersani, Leo, *Homos* (Cambridge, MA: Harvard University Press, 1995).

———, *Is the Rectum a Grave? And Other Essays* (Chicago; London: University of Chicago Press, 2010).

Bird, Phyllis, " 'To Play the Harlot': An Inquiry into an Old Testament Metaphor," in *Gender and Difference in Ancient Israel*, ed. Peggy Lynne Day (Minneapolis, MN: Fortress Press, 1989), 75–94.

————, "Prostitution in the Social World and the Religious Rhetoric of Ancient Israel," in *Prostitutes and Courtesans in the Ancient World*, eds. Christopher A. Faraone and Laura McClure (Madison: University of Wisconsin Press, 2006), 40–58.

Black, Max, "More About Metaphor," in *Metaphor and Thought*, ed. Andrew Ortony (Cambridge; New York: Cambridge University Press, 1979), 19–44.

Blount, Brian K., "The Witness of Active Resistance: The Ethics of Revelation in African American Perspective" in *From Every People and Nation: The Book of Revelation in Intercultural Perspective*, ed. David M. Rhoads (Minneapolis, MN: Fortress Press, 2005), 28–46.

Boer, Roland, *Criticism of Heaven: On Marxism and Theology* (Leiden; Boston: Brill, 2007).

————, *Knockin' on Heaven's Door: The Bible and Popular Culture* (London; New York: Routledge, 1999).

————, *Last Stop Before Antarctica: The Bible and Postcolonialism in Australia* (Sheffield, UK: Sheffield Academic Press, 2001).

————, *Marxist Criticism of the Bible* (London; New York: T&T Clark International, 2003).

————, *Rescuing the Bible*, Blackwell Manifestos (Malden; Oxford: Wiley-Blackwell, 2007).

————, *Secularism and Biblical Studies* (London; Oakville: Equinox Pub., 2010).

————, and Fernando F. Segovia, *The Future of the Biblical Past: Envisioning Biblical Studies on a Global Key* (Atlanta, GA: Society of Biblical Literature, 2012).

Boesak, Allan Aubrey, *Comfort and Protest: Reflections on the Apocalypse of John of Patmos*, 1st ed. (Philadelphia: Westminster Press, 1987).

Borón, Atilio, *Empire and Imperialism: A Critical Reading of Michael Hardt and Antonio Negri* [in Translated from the Spanish.] (London; New York: Zed Books, 2005).

Boykin, Keith, *Beyond the Down Low: Sex and Denial in Black America* (New York: Carroll & Graf, 2005).

Brown, Wendy, *Undoing the Demos: Neoliberalism's Stealth Revolution* (Brooklyn, NY: Zone Books/Near Futures, 2015).

Brueggemann, Walter, *Tradition for Crisis: A Study in Hosea* (Richmond: John Knox Press, 1968).

Callahan, Allen Dwight, "Babylon Boycott: The Book of Revelation," *Interpretation* 63, no. 1 (2009): 48–54.

Carey, Greg, "A Man's Choice: Wealth Imagery and the Two Cities of the Book of Revelation," in *A Feminist Companion to the Apocalypse of John*, ed. Amy-Jill Levine (London; New York: T&T Clark, 2009), 147–58.

Carter, Warren, "Accomodating 'Jezebel' and Withdrawing John: Negotiating Empire in Revelation Then and Now," *Interpretation* 63, no. 1 (2009): 32–47.

————, *John and Empire: Initial Explorations* (New York: T & T Clark, 2008).

————, *The Roman Empire and the New Testament: An Essential Guide*, Abingdon Essential Guides (Nashville: Abingdon Press, 2006).

Castelli, Elizabeth Anne, *Imitating Paul: A Discourse of Power* (Louisville: Westminster John Knox Press, 1991).

Cohen, Edward, "Free and Unfree Sexual Work: An Economic Analysis of Athenian Prostitution," in *Prostitutes and Courtesans in the Ancient World*, eds. Christopher A. Faraone and Laura McClure (Madison: University of Wisconsin Press, 2006).

Collins, John J., *The Bible After Babel: Historical Criticism in a Postmodern Age* (Grand Rapids, MI: W.B. Eerdmans 2005).

Comblin, José, "O Apocalipse De João E O Fim Do Mundo," *Estudos Biblicos* 59 (1998): 29–62.

Crowell, Bradley L., "Good Girl, Bad Girl: Foreign Women of the Deuteronomistic History in Postcolonial Perspective," *Biblical Interpretation* 21, no. 1 (2013): 1–18.

D'Emilio, John, "Capitalism and Sexual Identity," in *The Lesbian and Gay Studies Reader*, eds. Henry Abelove, Michèle Aina Barale, and David M. Halperin (New York: Routledge, 1993), 467–76.

Dardot, Pierre, and Christian Laval, *The New Way of the World: On Neoliberal Society* [in Translated from the French] (London; New York: Verso, 2013).

Dijk-Hemmes, Fokkelien van, "The Imagination of Power and the Power of Imagination: An Intertextual Analysis of Two Biblical Love Songs," *Journal for the Study of the Old Testament* no. 44 (1989): 75–88.

Dinshaw, Carolyn, *Getting Medieval: Sexualities and Communities, Pre- and Postmodern* (Durham, NC: Duke University Press, 1999).

Douglas, Mary, *Purity and Danger: An Analysis of Concept of Pollution and Taboo*, Routledge Classics (London; New York: Routledge, 2005).

Duff, Paul Brooks, *Who Rides the Beast? Prophetic Rivalry and the Rhetoric of Crisis in the Churches of the Apocalypse* (Oxford; New York: Oxford University Press, 2001).

Dworkin, Andrea, *Pornography: Men Possessing Women* (New York: Putnam, 1981).

Edelman, Lee, *No Future: Queer Theory and the Death Drive* (Durham, NC: Duke University Press, 2004).

Eribon, Didier, "Michel Foucault's Histories of Sexuality," *GLQ: A Journal of Lesbian and Gay Studies* 7, no. 1 (2001): 31–86.

Everhart, Janet S., "Jezebel: Framed by Eunuchs?" *Catholic Biblical Quarterly* 72, no. 4 (2010): 688–98.

Exum, J. Cheryl, *Fragmented Women: Feminist (Sub)Versions of Biblical Narratives*, 1st ed. (Valley Forge: Trinity Press International, 1993).

Fanon, Frantz, *The Wretched of the Earth*, 1st Evergreen ed. (New York: Grove Weidenfeld, 1991).

Fernández Ramírez, Dagoberto, "The Judgment of God on the Multinationals: Revelation 18," in *Subversive Scriptures: Revolutionary Readings of the Christian Bible in Latin America*, ed. Leif Vaage (Valley Forge: Trinity Press International, 1990), 55–74.

Fontaine, Carole R., "Response to 'Hosea'," in *A Feminist Companion to the Latter Prophets*, ed. Athalya Brenner (Sheffield, UK: Sheffield Academic Press, 1995), 60–9.

Foucault, Michel, "The Ethics of the Concern of the Self as a Practice of Freedom," in *Ethics: Subjectivity and Truth*, ed. Paul Rabinow (New York: New Press, 1997), 281–301.

———, *The History of Sexuality. Vol. 1: An Introduction* (New York: Vantage, 1990).

———, *The History of Sexuality. Vol. 2: The Use of Pleasure* (New York: Vintage Books, 1990).

———, *The History of Sexuality Vol. 3: The Care of the Self* (New York: Vintage Books, 2002).

———, "On the Genealogy of Ethics," in *Ethics: Subjectivity and Truth*, ed. Paul Rabinow (New York: New Press, 1997).

——, "The Subject of Power," *Critical Inquiry* 8, no. 4 (1982): 777–95.

——, Mauro Bertani, Alessandro Fontana, François Ewald, and David Macey, *Society Must Be Defended: Lectures at the Collège De France, 1975–76*, 1st ed. (New York: Picador, 2003).

——, Luther H. Martin, Huck Gutman, and Patrick H. Hutton, *Technologies of the Self: A Seminar with Michel Foucault* (Amherst: University of Massachusetts Press, 1988).

Foulkes, Ricardo, *El Apocalipsis De San Juan: Una Lectura Desde AméRica Latina* (Buenos Aires; Grand Rapids, MI: Nueva Creación; W.B. Eerdmans, 1989).

Fowl, Stephen E., "The Ethics of Interpretation, or What's Left Over After the Elimination of Meaning," in *Bible in Three Dimensions: Essays in Celebration of Forty Years of Biblical Studies in the University of Sheffield* (Sheffield, UK: Sheffield University Press, 1990), 379–98.

Fowler, Robert M., Edith Waldvogel Blumhofer, and Fernando F. Segovia, *New Paradigms for Bible Study: The Bible in the Third Millennium* (New York: T & T Clark International, 2004).

Fradenburg, L. O. Aranye, and Carla Freccero, *Premodern Sexualities* (New York: Routledge, 1995).

Freccero, Carla, *Queer/Early/Modern* (Durham, NC: Duke University Press, 2006).

——, "Queer Times," in *After Sex? On Writing Since Queer Theory*, eds. Janet E. Halley and Andrew Parker (Durham, NC: Duke University Press, 2011), 17–26.

Friesen, Steven J., *Imperial Cults and the Apocalypse of John: Reading Revelation in the Ruins* (Oxford; New York: Oxford University Press, 2001).

——, "Injustice or God's Will: Explanations of Poverty in Proto-Christian Texts," in *Christian Origins: People's History of Christianity*, ed. by Richard A. Horsley (Minneapolis, MN: Fortress Press, 2005), 240–60.

Frilingos, Christopher A., *Spectacles of Empire: Monsters, Martyrs, and the Book of Revelation*, Divinations (Philadelphia: University of Pennsylvania Press, 2004).

Gager, John G., *Kingdom and Community: The Social World of Early Christianity* (Englewood Cliffs: Prentice-Hall, 1975).

Gaines, Janet Howe, *Music in the Old Bones: Jezebel Through the Ages* (Carbondale: Southern Illinois University Press, 1999).

Glancy, Jennifer A., and Stephen D. Moore, "How Typical a Roman Prostitute Is Revelation's 'Great Whore'?" *Journal of Biblical Literature* 130, no. 3 (2011): 551–69.

González, Justo L., "Revelation: Clarity and Ambivalence: A Hispanic/Cuban American Perspective," in *From Every People and Nation: The Book of Revelation in Intercultural Perspective*, ed. David M. Rhoads (Minneapolis, MN: Fortress Press, 2005), 47–61.

Gorman, Michael J., *Reading Revelation Responsibly: Uncivil Worship and Witness: Following the Lamb into the New Creation* (Eugene: Cascade Books, 2011).

Gottwald, Norman K., "From Tribal Existence to Empire: The Socio-Historical Context for the Rise of the Hebrew Prophets," in *God and Capitalism: A Prophetic Critique of Market Economy*, eds. Norman K. Gottwald, J. Mark Thomas, and Vern Visick (Madison: A-R Editions, 1991).

Guest, Deryn, Robert E. Goss, Mona West, and Thomas Bohache, *The Queer Bible Commentary* (London: SCM, 2006).

Halperin, David M., *How to Do the History of Homosexuality* (Chicago: University of Chicago Press, 2002).

————, *Saint Foucault: Towards a Gay Hagiography* (New York: Oxford University Press, 1995).

Haraway, Donna, "The Persistence of Vision," in *The Visual Culture Reader*, ed. Nicholas Mirzoeff (London; New York: Routledge, 1998), 677–84.

Hardt, Michael, *Multitude: War and Democracy in the Age of Empire* (New York: Penguin Press, 2004).

Hardt, Michael, and Antonio Negri, *Commonwealth* (Cambridge: Belknap Press of Harvard University Press, 2009).

————, *Empire* (Cambridge, MA: Harvard University Press, 2000).

Harland, Philip A., "Honouring the Emperor or Assailing the Beast: Participation in Civic Life Among Associations (Jewish, Christian and Other) in Asia Minor and the Apocalypse of John," *Journal for the Study of the New Testament* no. 77 (2000): 99–121.

Harper, Kyle, "Porneia: The Making of a Christian Sexual Norm," *Journal of Biblical Literature* 131, no. 2 (2012): 363–83.

Hennessy, Rosemary, *Profit and Pleasure: Sexual Identities in Late Capitalism* (New York: Routledge, 2000).

Hidalgo, Jacqueline M., *Revelation in Aztlán: Scriptures, Utopias, and the Chicano Movement* (New York: Palgrave Macmillan, 2016).

Hill, Craig A., *Human Sexuality: Personality and Social Psychological Perspectives* (Los Angeles: Sage, 2008).

Holt, Else Kragelund, " '. . . Urged on by His Wife Jezebel': A Literary Reading of 1 Kgs 18 in Context," *Scandinavian Journal of the Old Testament* 9, no. 1 (1995): 83–96.

Hornsby, Teresa J., " 'Israel Has Become a Worthless Thing': Re-Reading Gomer in Hosea 1–3," *Journal for the Study of the Old Testament* no. 82 (1999): 115–28.

————, and Ken Stone, *Bible Trouble Queer Reading at the Boundaries of Biblical Scholarship* (Atlanta: Society of Biblical Literature, 2011).

Huber, Lynn R., *Like a Bride Adorned: Reading Metaphor in John's Apocalypse* (New York: T&T Clark International, 2007).

————, *Thinking and Seeing Women in Revelation* (London; New York: Bloomsbury, 2013).

————, "Gazing at the Whore: Reading Revelation Queerly," in *Bible Trouble: Queer Reading at the Boundaries of Biblical Scholarship*, eds. Ken Stone and Teresa J. Hornsby (Atlanta: Society of Biblical Literature, 2011), 301–20.

Huffer, Lynne, *Mad for Foucault: Rethinking the Foundations of Queer Theory* (New York: Columbia University Press, 2010).

Hylen, Susan, "Metaphor Matters: Violence and Ethics in Revelation," *The Catholic Biblical Quarterly* 73, no. 4 (2011): 777–96.

Joshel, Sandra R., "Female Desire and the Discourse of Empire: Tacitus's Messalina," *Signs* 21, no. 1 (1995): 50–82.

Kaden, David A., "Foucault, Feminism, and Liberationist Religion: Discourse, Power, and the Politics of Interpretation in the Feminist Emancipatory Project of Elisabeth Schüssler Fiorenza," *Neotestamentica* 46, no. 1 (2012): 92–114.

Karras, Ruth Mazo, *Common Women: Prostitution and Sexuality in Medieval England* (New York: Oxford University Press, 1996).

Kim, Jean K., " 'Uncovering Her Wickedness': An Inter(Con)Textual Reading of Revelation 17 from a Postcolonial Feminist Perspective," *Journal for the Study of the New Testament* 73 (1999): 61–81.

Knust, Jennifer Wright, *Abandoned to Lust: Sexual Slander and Ancient Christianity* (New York: Columbia University Press, 2006).

Koester, Craig R., "Revelation's Visionary Challenge to Ordinary Empire," *Interpretation* 63, no. 1 (2009): 5–18.

———, "Roman Slave Trade and the Critique of Babylon in Revelation 18," *The Catholic Biblical Quarterly* 70, no. 4 (2008): 766–86.

Koljevic, Bogdana, *Twenty-First Century Biopolitics* (Austria: Peter Lang GmbH, 2015).

Kraybill, J. Nelson, *Apocalypse and Allegiance: Worship, Politics, and Devotion in the Book of Revelation* (Grand Rapids, MI: Brazos Press, 2010).

———, *Imperial Cult and Commerce in John's Apocalypse*, Journal for the Study of the New Testament Supplement Series (Sheffield, UK: Sheffield Academic Press, 1996).

Kulick, Don, *Travesti: Sex, Gender, and Culture Among Brazilian Transgendered Prostitutes*, Worlds of Desire (Chicago: University of Chicago Press, 1998).

Lamarche, Pierre David Sherman, and Max Rosenkrantz, *Reading Negri: Marxism in the Age of Empire*, Volume 3 of Creative Marxism (Chicago: Open Court, 2011).

Larkins, Sherry, and Cathy Reback, "Maintaining a Heterosexual Identity: Sexual Meanings Among a Sample of Heterosexually Identified Men Who Have Sex with Men," *Archives of Sexual Behavior* 39, no. 3 (2010): 766–73.

Lopez, Davina C., *Apostle to the Conquered: Reimagining Paul's Mission* (Minneapolis, MN: Fortress Press, 2008).

Lowe, Donald M., *The Body in Late-Capitalist USA* (Durham, NC: Duke University Press, 1995).

Macwilliam, Stuart, *Queer Theory and the Prophetic Marriage Metaphor in the Hebrew Bible*, Bibleworld (Sheffield, UK; Oakville, CT: Equinox Pub., 2011).

Maier, Harry O., "Staging the Gaze: Early Christian Apocalypses and Narrative Self-Representation," *Harvard Theological Review* 90, no. 2 (1997): 131–54.

Malina, Bruce J., *The New Testament World: Insights from Cultural Anthropology*, 3rd ed. (Louisville: Westminster John Knox Press, 2001).

Marshall, John W., "Gender and Empire: Sexualized Violence in John's Anti-Imperial Apocalypse," in *A Feminist Companion to the Apocalypse of John*, eds. Amy-Jill Levine and Maria Mayo Robbins (London; New York: T&T Clark, 2009), 17–32.

Martin, Clarice, "Polishing the Unclouded Mirror: A Womanist Reading of Revelation 18:13," in *From Every People and Nation: The Book of Revelation in Intercultural Perspective*, ed. David M. Rhoads (Minneapolis, MN: Fortress Press, 2005), 82–109.

Martin, Dale B., *The Corinthian Body* (New Haven: Yale University Press, 1995).

———, *Pedagogy of the Bible: An Analysis and Proposal*, 1st ed. (Louisville: Westminster John Knox Press, 2008).

Matthews, Mark D., *Riches, Poverty, and the Faithful: Perspectives on Wealth in the Second Temple Period and the Apocalypse of John*, Society for New Testament Studies Monograph Series (Cambridge: Cambridge University Press, 2013).

McClintock, Anne, *Imperial Leather: Race, Gender, and Sexuality in the Colonial Contest* (New York: Routledge, 1995).

McKinlay, Judith E., "Rahab: A Hero/Ine?" *Biblical Interpretation* 7, no. 1 (1999): 44–57.

———, *Reframing Her: Biblical Women in Postcolonial Focus* (Sheffield, UK: Sheffield Phoenix Press, 2004).

Medina, José, "Toward a Foucaultian Epistemology of Resistance: Counter-Memory, Epistemic Friction, and Guerrilla Pluralism," *Foucault Studies* no. 12 (2011): 9–35.

Menéndez-Antuña, Luis, "The Queer Art of Biblical Reading: Matthew 25:31–46 (*Caritas Christiana*) Through *Caritas Romana*," *Journal of Religious Ethics* 45, no. 4 (2017): 732–59.

Menon, Madhavi, *Unhistorical Shakespeare: Queer Theory in Shakespearean Literature and Film*, 1st ed. (New York: Palgrave Macmillan, 2008).

Michaels, J. Ramsey, *Revelation* (Downers Grove: InterVarsity Press, 1997).

Moore, Stephen D., "The Beatific Vision as a Posing Exhibition: Revelation's Hypermasculine Deity," *Journal for the Study of the New Testament* 18, no. 60 (1996): 27–55.

———, *Empire and Apocalypse: Postcolonialism and the New Testament*, Bible in the Modern World v. 12 (Sheffield, UK: Sheffield Phoenix Press, 2006).

———, *God's Gym: Divine Male Bodies of the Bible* (New York: Routledge, 1996).

———, "Metonymies of Empire: Sexual Humiliation and Gender Masquerade in the Book of Revelation," in *Postcolonial Interventions: Essays in Honor of R. S. Sugirtharajah* (Sheffield, UK: Sheffield Phoenix Press, 2009), 71–97.

———, "A Modest Manifesto for New Testament Literary Criticism: How to Interface with a Literary Studies Field That Is Post-Literary, Post-Theoretical, and Post-Methodological," *Biblical Interpretation* 15, no. 1 (2007): 1–25.

———, "Questions of Biblical Ambivalence and Authority Under a Tree Outside Delhi; or, the Postcolonial and the Postmodern," in *Postcolonial Biblical Criticism: Interdisciplinary Intersections*, eds. Stephen D. Moore and Fernando F. Segovia (London; New York: T & T Clark International, 2007), 79–96.

———, and ebrary Inc., *God's Beauty Parlor and Other Queer Spaces in and Around the Bible* (Stanford, CA: Stanford University Press, 2001), http://site.ebrary.com/lib/yale/Doc?id=10042833.

———, and Yvonne Sherwood, *The Invention of the Biblical Scholar: A Critical Manifesto* (Minneapolis, MN: Fortress Press, 2011).

Morris, Leon, *Revelation: An Introduction and Commentary* (Downers Grove: IVP Academic, 2007).

Mounce, Robert H., *The Book of Revelation*, Rev. ed. (Grand Rapids, MI: W.B. Eerdmans, 1997).

Moxnes, Halvor, "Asceticism and Christian Identity in Antiquity: A Dialogue with Foucault and Paul," *Journal for the Study of the New Testament* 26, no. 1 (2003): 3–29.

Murphy, Timothy S., and Abdul-Karim Mustapha, *Resistance in Practice: The Philosophy of Antonio Negri* (London: Pluto Press, 2005).

Nairn, Tom, "Make for the Boondocks," *London Review of Books* 27, no. 9 (2005): 11–14.

Negri, Antonio, *Reflections on Empire* (Cambridge, MA; Malden, UK: Polity Press, 2008).

Neusner, Jacob, *The Idea of Purity in Ancient Judaism* (Leiden: Brill, 1973).

Neyrey, Jerome H., "Jesus, Gender, and the Gospel of Matthew," in *New Testament Masculinities* (Atlanta: Soc of Biblical Literature, 2003), 43–66.

———, *Paul, in Other Words: A Cultural Reading of His Letters*, 1st ed. (Louisville: Westminster/John Knox Press, 1990).

Nicolet-Anderson, Valérie, *Constructing the Self: Thinking with Paul and Michel Foucault* (Tübingen: Mohr Siebeck, 2012).

O'Leary, Timothy, *Foucault: The Art of Ethics* (London; New York: Continuum, 2002).

Olson, Daniel C., " 'Those Who Have Not Defiled Themselves with Women': Revelation 14:4 and the Book of Enoch," *Catholic Biblical Quarterly* 59, no. 3 (1997): 492–510.

Osborne, Grant R., *Revelation: Baker Exegetical Commentary on the New Testament* (Grand Rapids, MI: Baker Academic, 2002).

Pippin, Tina, *Death and Desire: The Rhetoric of Gender in the Apocalypse of John*, 1st ed. (Louisville: Westminster/John Knox Press, 1992).

———, "Eros and the End: Reading for Gender in the Apocalypse of John," *Semeia* no. 59 (1992): 193–210.

———, "The Heroine and the Whore: Fantasy and the Female in the Apocalypse of John," in *From Every People and Nation: The Book of Revelation in Intercultural Perspective*, ed. David M. Rhoads (Minneapolis, MN: Fortress Press, 2005), 127–45.

Pomper, Philip, "The History and Theory of Empires," *History and Theory* 44, no. 4 (2005): 1–27.

Price, S.R.F., *Rituals and Power: The Roman Imperial Cult in Asia Minor* (Cambridge; New York: Cambridge University Press, 1984).

Provan, Iain W., "Foul Spirits, Fornication and Finance: Revelation 18 from an Old Testament Perspective," *Journal for the Study of the New Testament* 64 (1996): 81–100.

Puar, Jasbir K., *Terrorist Assemblages: Homonationalism in Queer Times*, Next Wave (Durham, NC: Duke University Press, 2007).

Rana, Junaid Akram, *Terrifying Muslims: Race and Labor in the South Asian Diaspora* (Durham, NC: Duke University Press, 2011).

Rhoads, David M., *From Every People and Nation: The Book of Revelation in Intercultural Perspective* (Minneapolis, MN: Fortress Press, 2005).

Rhodes, R.A.W., *Understanding Governance: Policy Networks, Governance, Reflexivity, and Accountability*, Public Policy and Management (Buckingham; Philadelphia: Open University Press, 1997).

Richard, Pablo, *Apocalypse: A People's Commentary on the Book of Revelation*, The Bible & Liberation Series (Maryknoll: Orbis Books, 1995).

Riegner, Irene E., *The Vanishing Hebrew Harlot: The Adventures of the Hebrew Stem Znh*, Studies in Biblical Literature (New York: Peter Lang, 2009).

Rossing, Barbara R., *The Choice Between Two Cities: Whore, Bride, and Empire in the Apocalypse* (Harrisburg: Trinity Press International, 1999).

Rowlett, Lori, "Disney's Pocahontas and Joshua's Rahab in Postcolonial Perspective," in *Culture, Entertainment, and the Bible*, ed. George Aichele (Sheffield, UK: Sheffield Academic Press, 2000), 66–75.

Royalty, Robert M., *The Streets of Heaven: The Ideology of Wealth in the Apocalypse of John* (Macon: Mercer University Press, 1998).

Runions, Erin, *The Babylon Complex: Theopolitical Fantasies of War, Sex, and Sovereignty*, 1st ed. (New York: Fordham University Press, 2014).

———, "From Disgust to Humor: Rahab's Queer Affect," *Postscripts* 4, no. 1 (2008): 41–69.

Schüssler Fiorenza, Elisabeth, *The Book of Revelation: Justice and Judgment*, 2nd ed. (Minneapolis, MN: Fortress Press, 1998).

———, *Democratizing Biblical Studies: Toward an Emancipatory Educational Space*, 1st ed. (Louisville: Westminster John Knox Press, 2009).

———, *Jesus and the Politics of Interpretation* (New York: Continuum, 2000).

———, *The Power of the Word: Scripture and the Rhetoric of Empire* (Minneapolis, MN: Fortress Press, 2007).

———, *Revelation: Vision of a Just World* (Minneapolis, MN: Fortress Press, 1991).

———, *Rhetoric and Ethic: The Politics of Biblical Studies* (Minneapolis, MN: Fortress Press, 1999).

———, *Sharing Her Word: Feminist Biblical Interpretation in Context* (Boston: Beacon Press, 1998).

Sedgwick, Eve Kosofsky, *Epistemology of the Closet* (New York; London: Harvester Wheatsheaf, 1991).

Segovia, Fernando F., "Criticism in Critical Times: Reflections on Vision and Task," *Journal of Biblical Literature* 134, no. 1 (2015): 6–29.

———, "Toward a Hermeneutics of the Diaspora: A Hermeneutics of Otherness and Engagement," in *Reading from This Place (Vol. 1): Social Location and Biblical Interpretation in the United States*, eds. Fernando F. Segovia and Mary Ann Tolbert (Minneapolis, MN: Fortress, 1995), 57–74.

Sharp, Carolyn J., *Irony and Meaning in the Hebrew Bible*, Indiana Studies in Biblical Literature (Bloomington: Indiana University Press, 2009).

Sherwood, Yvonne, *The Prostitute and the Prophet: Hosea's Marriage in Literary-Theoretical Perspective* (Sheffield, UK: Sheffield Academic Press, 1996).

Siegel, Karolynn, Eric W. Schrimshaw, Helen-Maria Lekas, and Jeffrey T. Parsons, "Sexual Behaviors of Non-Gay Identified Non-Disclosing Men Who Have Sex with Men and Women," *Archives of Sexual Behavior* 37, no. 5 (2008): 732–34.

Smalley, Stephen S., *The Revelation to John: A Commentary on the Greek Text of the Apocalypse* (Downers Grove: InterVarsity Press, 2005).

Smart, Barry, *Michel Foucault* (London; New York: E. Horwood; Tavistock Publications, 1985).

Spivak, Gayatri Chakravorty, "Can the Subaltern Speak?" in *Marxism and the Interpretation of Culture*, eds. Cary Nelson and Lawrence Grossberg (Urbana: University of Illinois Press, 1988), 271–313.

St. Clair Darden, Lynne, *Scripturalizing Revelation: An African American Postcolonial Reading of Empire* (Atlanta: Society of Biblical Literature, 2015).

Stek, John H., "Rahab of Canaan and Israel: The Meaning of Joshua 2," *Calvin Theological Journal* 37, no. 1 (2002): 28–48.

Stone, Ken, "Lovers and Raisin Cakes: Food, Sex and Divine Insecurity in Hosea," in *Queer Commentary and the Hebrew Bible*, ed. Ken Stone (Sheffield, UK: Sheffield Academic Press, 2001).

———, *Queer Commentary and the Hebrew Bible*, Journal for the Study of the Old Testament. Supplement Series 334 (Cleveland, OH: Pilgrim Press, 2001).

Taylor, Charles, *Sources of the Self: The Making of the Modern Identity* (Cambridge, MA: Harvard University Press, 1989).

Thimmes, Pamela, " 'Teaching and Beguiling My Servants': The Letter to Thyatira (Rev. 2.18–29)," in *A Feminist Companion to the Apocalypse of John*, ed. Amy-Jill Levine (London; New York: T&T Clark, 2009), 69–87.

Thompson, Leonard L., *The Book of Revelation: Apocalypse and Empire* (New York: Oxford University Press, 1990).

Traub, Valerie, *The Renaissance of Lesbianism in Early Modern England*, Cambridge Studies in Renaissance Literature and Culture (Cambridge; New York: Cambridge University Press, 2002).

Ure, Michael, "Senecan Moods: Foucault and Nietzsche on the Art of the Self," *Foucault Studies* 19–52, no. 4 (2007).

Vaka'uta, Nāsili, "Border Crossing/Body Whoring: Rereading Rahab of Jericho with Native Women," in *Postcolonialism and the Hebrew Bible: The Next Step*, ed. Roland Boer (Atlanta: Society of Biblical Literature, 2013), 143–56.

Vander Stichele, Caroline, "Re-Membering the Whore: The Fate of Babylon According to Revelation 17.16," in *A Feminist Companion to the Apocalypse of John*, ed. Amy-Jill Levine (London; New York: T&T Clark, 2009), 106–20.

Wainwright, Arthur William, *Mysterious Apocalypse: Interpreting the Book of Revelation* (Nashville: Abingdon Press, 1993).

Weems, Renita J., *Battered Love: Marriage, Sex, and Violence in the Hebrew Prophets* (Minneapolis, MN: Fortress Press, 1995).

Williams, Craig A., *Roman Homosexuality: Ideologies of Masculinity in Classical Antiquity* (New York: Oxford University Press, 1998).

Wilson, Brittany E., *Unmanly Men: Refigurations of Masculinity in Luke-Acts* (New York: Oxford University Press, 2015).

Winkler, John J., *The Constraints of Desire: The Anthropology of Sex and Gender in Ancient Greece* (New York: Routledge, 1990).

Wyatt, Stephanie, "Jezebel, Elijah, and the Widow of Zarephath: A Ménage À Trois That Estranges the Holy and Makes the Holy the Strange," *Journal for the Study of the Old Testament* 36, no. 4 (2012): 435–58.

Yarbro Collins, Adela, *The Combat Myth in the Book of Revelation: Harvard Dissertations in Religion*, Harvard Dissertations in Religion (Missoula, MT: Published by Scholars Press for Harvard theological review, 1976).

———, *Crisis and Catharsis: The Power of the Apocalypse*, 1st ed. (Philadelphia: Westminster Press, 1984).

———, "Feminine Symbolism in the Book of Revelation," *Biblical Interpretation* 1, no. 1 (F 1993): 20–33.

———, "Persecution and Vengeance in the Book of Revelation," in *Apocalypticism in the Mediterranean World and the Near East* (Tübingen: Mohr Siebeck, 1983), 729–49.

———, "Women's History and the Book of Revelation," in *Society of Biblical Literature 1987 Seminar Papers*, ed. Kent Harold Richards (Atlanta, GA: Scholars Press, 1987), 80–91.

Yee, Gale A., " 'She Is Not My Wife and I Am Not Her Husband': A Materialist Analysis of Hosea 1–2," *Biblical Interpretation* 9, no. 4 (2001): 345–83.

Index